DENOMINATIONS—

HOW WE GOT THEM

Denominations—
How We Got Them

STANLEY I. STUBER

Condensed and revised from
How We Got Our Denominations

ASSOCIATION PRESS   •   New York

DENOMINATIONS—HOW WE GOT THEM

Copyright © 1958, 1959 by
National Board of
Young Men's Christian Associations

Association Press, 291 Broadway, New York 7, N. Y.

Price, 50 cents

Library of Congress catalog card number: 58-6474

Printed in the United States of America

CONTENTS

INTRODUCTION

Christians of all denominations are today making an earnest attempt to discover, through the pages of the New Testament and the early church fathers, the true meaning of the Church Universal and their own relationship to it. This concern about relationships brings new attention to the origin and meaning of our denominations.

This book, which is a revision and condensation of my earlier full-length book *How We Got Our Denominations,* is meant to be a primer-type, straightforward telling of the basic facts regarding church history, with special emphasis upon a selected group of American churches. This is done in the simplest style and in the fewest numbers of words possible.

Why are there so many denominations? Looking briefly in these pages at how we got them helps to answer the question. But, though accepting denominations as valid instruments of the Kingdom, reflective Christians of all denominations may ponder how we can demonstrate our *oneness* in Christ.

STANLEY I. STUBER

Kansas City, Missouri

1. THE EARLY CHURCH

THE BIRTHDAY OF THE CHURCH

When was the birthday of the Church? It is impossible to say just when, for the Church was in existence before the day of Pentecost. But because so many consider it the day the Christian church was first realized, and since it was a red-letter day in its history, the day of Pentecost is usually regarded as the birthday of the Church. (Of course, the disciples were not called Christians at this time.)

It was the seventh Sunday after the resurrection of Jesus; the disciples were waiting for the coming of the Holy Spirit which Jesus had promised them. The upper chamber, probably where the Last Supper was eaten, served as their meeting place. Here, grouped together with a common purpose, this little band of believers had begun to develop a strong bond of unity. Once they had been disciples of the Master; now they were brothers in Christ.

Here is opened before us the Christian Age. At this time the followers of Christ received a new sense

of their oneness with God and with one another. It
was the day when the evangelistic activity of the
Christian church began and when the disciples first
realized that their mission was to be witness bearers
of the living Lord throughout the then known world.

JESUS ACCEPTED AS THE MESSIAH

The followers of the Master were now ready to
go a step farther than the Jewish church ever dared
to go. They accepted Jesus as the Messiah. Here
lies the secret of the enthusiasm of primitive Christianity. The belief that Jesus rose from the grave
colored the whole life of this period and gave the
disciples the triumphant power of the message which
they proclaimed. By accepting Jesus as the Messiah,
the Christian church received a more abundant
life.

GROWTH THROUGH PERSECUTION

The murder of Stephen was the beginning of a
period of persecution against the Christians. They
were dragged to prison, and their meeting places
were destroyed. The only practical thing these as-
sailed Christians could do was to take refuge in
flight or to resist. But since hardship or persecution
often tends to make for strength, the Church received
much good from this struggle. It helped:

To purge out the false or half hearted members.

To end the unrealistic practice of sharing all
things in common.

To spread far and wide the Christian teaching.

To develop leaders who were earnest in the
spirit and instructed in the faith.

To cause a growth in the knowledge of Christian
living, organization, and church worship.

THE ROMAN GOVERNMENT

During the first half of the apostolic age (the
period when Peter and the other disciples began
their ministry after the crucifixion and resurrection
of Jesus) the Christians enjoyed a short period of
peace, except for a few cases of ill-treatment by the
Jews. The Roman Government used them justly,
though perhaps somewhat contemptuously. Later
the Romans took up the persecution, and strange
as it may seem rulers like Trajan and Marcus Aure-
lius were among the worst persecutors, while some
of the most infamous emperors were indifferent and
sometimes even favorable to Christianity. The persecution of the early days was only spasmodic and
limited, having no backing from the Roman Government, while the persecutions of a later date were
more general and conducted under the command
of the emperor himself. The severity of the persecution depended upon the whims and feelings of each
individual emperor.

Why the Christians Were Persecuted

"Does not the Emperor punish you justly?" Celsus, a Latin encyclopedist, asked the Christians. "Should all do like you, he would be left alone— there would be none to defend him." This was the common belief held among the Romans. They began to fear this secret body of irresistible people who were called Christians. And why should they not have cause to fear? Christianity caused trouble wherever it went! It was opposed to the whole governmental, social, and religious systems of Rome. It broke up homes, setting the husband against the wife, the children against their parents, the slave against his master. It caused the traders and priests of the temple a loss of profits, for these Christians worshiped with neither image nor shrine. It would have nothing to do with the licentious and cruel amusements of the Romans. It refused the duty of a loyal citizen and would hold no office. It objected to all military service and refused to worship the emperor. As its meetings were held at night, with both sexes present, they were mistaken for carnivals of lust, where, as the Romans thought, their offspring of passion were sacrificed to their one god. Also, it was intolerant of all other religions. All this tended to make the Romans look upon Christians as the worst of degenerates, who should be cast from society. No punishment could be too severe for these people called Christians.

THE RESULTS OF THE PERSECUTION

The results of the persecution can be summed up in these six points:

It "advertised" Christianity and won sympathy, which caused it to grow.

It created an intense devotion among the Christians.

It proved the truth of Christianity.

It produced efficient organizations and leaders.

It produced a group of extraordinary literary defenders, such as the apologists and letter writers.

It furnished an example for later persecutions.

VICTORY—CHRISTIANITY WINS

During this period Christianity made great progress. The persecution had won many converts to the new faith. Although it had no Christian government to protect or foster it, Christianity soon grew into manhood. No one knows the number of Christians at this time, for very few records have been left and these give much too low an estimate of the total number. But after careful investigation it is thought that there must have been between 30,000,000 and 100,000,000. McGlothlin says that "by the end of the period, perhaps as much as one-tenth of the population of the empire was Christian." This shows that Christianity was getting a very strong foothold in the Empire. Pagan Rome was giving way to the new faith.

Constantine, who had been dramatically converted to Christianity during a battle against Maxentius at the Milvian Bridge (A.D. 312), did much to establish the Universal Church. He was the first Roman ruler to give Christianity protection by law. He converted temples into churches and appointed special times and places for worship. He instigated laws which improved the condition of women, lessened the rigors of slavery, and otherwise reflected the spirit of Christianity. Thus the Christians became an important part of the Roman government—their Church was now the State-Church.

There is no doubt that Christianity would have gained a victory even if Constantine had not appeared as its champion. It was growing stronger each day, for it was the religion of Truth. Nothing could stop its advance. Christianity has been and always will be a "conquering world religion."

WHAT THE STATE DEMANDED OF THE CHURCH

Since the State was the means by which Christianity won its victory, it wished to share in the management of the Church. Now that new power had come to the State, it grew strong once more. Many of the clergy were given high offices in the government. Great sums of money were given for the building of new churches and charity. Everything was done on a large scale. Christianity was made the popular religion of the State.

Though, on the surface, it might seem that the Church was free and powerful, yet, at the same time, it was shut fast in a prison made with its own hands. With freedom from persecution came something far worse than the severest persecution, that is, moral decay. Truly, the Church was free from the fears of the sword, but it was not free to rule its own household. It became in too many ways merely a tool for the ambitions of the selfish and immoral rulers of the State. Using it as a tool the State demanded from it:

> The right to administer ecclesiastical law.
>
> The right to call all general councils and to confirm their actions.
>
> The right to elect all bishops of important sees.
>
> The right of supreme judge in the spiritual courts.
>
> A deciding vote in all dogmatic controversies.

HEADQUARTERS OF THE STATE-CHURCH

The Church at Rome grew very strong. It was situated at the center of the great empire and at a

time when it was the mistress of the world. Paul
saw great hopes for this Church of Rome, for it
naturally seemed to have great power and influence.
But no doubt Paul would have been very disap-
pointed in it if he could have visited it during this
period. It had taken on the organization of the
Empire, and after the State and Church had become
one, it became its servant. Thus the capital of the
Empire became the capital of the State-Church.

PERILS OF THE NEW ORDER

This unnatural union of Church and State had
many bad effects upon the true spirit of Christianity.
It was now very different from the simple religion
which Jesus taught. In organization it was no longer
a democracy, but an absolute monarchy. It was now
no struggling Church, but a mighty Church of gran-
deur, a power factor in society, industry, and education.

But as short cuts to success are always unwise, so
it was in this case. The object of Christianity was
to establish the kingdom of God in the hearts of
men. This could be done only step by step, through
kindly living and loving service.

In her great success the Church forgot almost
entirely about noble living. This was fatal to her
spiritual life. From this period to the Reformation,
the Church grew from bad to worse, until finally it

was preserved and rescued from its corruption by Martin Luther.

Some results of this new order of the State-Church were these:

A half-converted mass of heathen were added to the Church.

The Church became a center for worldliness and secular glory.

The Church became the slave of selfish and ambitious statesmen.

The Church was limited in its freedom.

2. DECLINE AND REFORMATION

THE COMING OF THE BARBARIANS

As early as A.D. 375, the people from the north began to migrate and invade the Roman Empire. In 476 the line of western emperors came to an end. At the opening of the sixth century the Ostrogoths had settled in Italy, the Franks in Gaul, the Anglo-Saxons in Britain, the Visigoths in Spain, and the Vandals in northern Africa.

It was the Frankish king, Clovis, who laid the foundation for what afterward became the empire of Charlemagne or Charles the Great. He, like most of the invaders, became a Christian, and as a result of this a close relationship between the Church and the Frankish dominions was formed. Although for a while after the death of Clovis conditions sank to a very low ebb, they were revived again under Pippin (687). His son, Charles Martel (715 to 741), for political reasons, greatly aided the Church and promoted many missionary and reformatory works in western Germany. When the Lombards began their invasion of Italy, the pope called on Charles Martel for aid, but all was in vain. So the pope crowned Pippin the Short (754), who had been wanting this kingly title, and with the aid of this general the Lombards were defeated and Rome saved. Thus began the Holy Roman Empire, which played so big a part in medieval history.

THE "STATE OF GOD"

It was through Charlemagne that the old line of Roman Caesars was revived in Europe. The Roman Empire had died at the hands of the invaders from the north and the Byzantine Empire of the East had gone far into decline. But the Roman Church still lived on. The pope still had the title of "Pontifex Maximus" and was not ready yet to give it up.

Christianity at this stage had lost most of its vision of the kingdom of Heaven, for it was greatly blinded by its task of reviving Roman ascendancy which it thought of as its inheritance. As a result of this, it had become a political body which used its members to further its material ends.

During the period following the death of Charlemagne, there was a rapid decline in the empire. His son, Louis the Pious, was wholly unfit for the task left by Charlemagne. His sons plotted against him and, at his death, the empire was divided between them by the Treaty of Verdun in 843. As the empire thus declined, the papacy grew in power. The popes showed themselves the strongest men of the time.

The papacy was now the only well-organized system of government in the Middle Ages. Everything had to bow before it.

SINS OF THE CHURCH

The monks and priests had yielded to the temptation of wealth and luxury. As the Latin language was alone used in connection with the Church, the mass of the people in the Germanic lands were totally ignorant of the Bible and the ideals of it. It was believed that the blessing of God could be purchased by gifts of money, and this belief was worked to its fullest degree by the selfish priests. Thus the system of indulgences was established. This permitted the people to make certain payments in order to be relieved from punishment of committed sins.

As the priests were not of the highest spiritual type and sometimes quite ignorant, conditions grew to be very serious. Finally some of the higher-minded laity and clergy did rise up in rebellion against such actions. They were the preservers of society during these dark ages. If it had not been for these few, who still held to the true and the beautiful, real Christianity would have been lost during this period.

DEFECTIVE PIETY

As the Church lost its spiritual vision and purity, it sought to cover up its sins by the use of outward and physical forms. There developed, therefore, at this time such manifestations as penances, indulgences, masses for the dead, ordeals, pilgrimages, and confessions. But they were only dead forms, invented to take the place of the slower and the harder way to salvation. The freshness and saving power of the Master's spirit was not contained in them. They knew him not.

But we should not think that all the Christians of this period were hopeless. There were many noble men in the Church; but they were overpowered.

DREAMS OF BETTER THINGS

Between the councils for reform and the Reformation is a period called the Renaissance—a time nations began to realize that they were alive and that life was really worth living. Browning's lines express the new attitude: "How good is man's life, the mere living! How fit to employ all the heart and the soul and the senses forever in joy!"

The change was from "otherworldliness" to "worldliness," used in the best sense of the term. The discovery of America, the return to classical scholarship, the paintings of Raphael, the plays of Shakespeare, the discovery that the world revolves about the sun, the printing of books, and other events were not the greatest things which happened during this period. Greater than all these were revival of the human mind and spirit, the realization of man's possibilities, the awakening to the beauties of the world, and the appreciation of the joys in this present life.

THE GREAT REFORMER

Martin Luther was born November 10, 1483, in Eisleben, Germany. His parents were simple people, with a good amount of piety, and they gave him the best schooling that Germany could afford. He had a brilliant record as a student and planned, upon his graduation from the University of Erfurt, to practice law. But his plans were destroyed by the sudden death of a friend and by a narrow escape from death which caused him such anxiety for his soul's salvation that he entered a monastery of Augustinian hermits in Erfurt, July, 1505. He was such a scholarly monk that he soon gained wide recognition. In 1512 he became a lecturer on the Bible and the district vicar of eleven monasteries. Later he became professor in the University of Wittenberg.

In 1512 he was sent to Rome on business by the Augustinian order and was startled by the loose living and lifeless religion which he found there. On his return he applied himself to the study of the Bible and began teaching justification by faith, as found in the "Epistle to the Romans" and "the

Epistle to the Galatians." When Johann Tetzel, a Dominican monk, came into his district selling indulgences, that the great St. Peter's might be built, Luther rose up in rebellion and nailed "ninety-five theses" on the castle church at Wittenberg (October, 1517), attacking indulgences, both in practice and in theory. But it was not his purpose to have the practice abandoned altogether, only to restore it to its former position. The theses were merely intended for academic debate. Instead, they stirred up the people of the whole nation and, in the end, changed the entire course of the Christian church. Luther then became the center of a mighty upheaval of religious thought, which soon got beyond his control and pushed forward in wild confusion over all Europe. As a result Luther was summoned to Rome, but taking the advice of the Elector of Saxony he refused to go. In 1520 he was excommunicated by the Church and in 1521 he was placed under the ban of the Empire by the Diet of Worms. During the time which he was under this ban he worked on a translation of the Bible. The work was finished in 1534. He gave the German people a translation of the Scriptures which was idiomatic and very readable, insomuch that it largely determined the form of speech of future German literature. In all the history of translation there is no achievement that can equal this. It was the first translation to be made directly from the Greek text into ordinary, everyday language.

Luther is therefore the great hero of the Protestant world.

"THE PROTESTANT POPE," JOHN CALVIN

John Calvin was born in 1509 at Noyon, France, of an influential family. He received a very fine education and showed remarkable abilities as a student. At an early age he held positions in the Church and at one time prepared for the law. His conversion was sudden and lasting. In 1533 he was arrested as a reformer but escaped to Geneva. There he met the reformer Farel in 1536, who determined to a great extent his future. Remaining at Geneva he soon became its undisputed master. McGlothin described Geneva thus:

"From one of the gayest and most reckless cities of Europe, Geneva was transformed into the soberest and most law-abiding and serious city in the world. It was virtually a theocracy. The church completely dominated the life of the entire community."

In 1559 Calvin founded the University of Geneva, which became the leading theological school of Europe, and sent its graduates to Scotland, Germany, and Italy. Thus Calvinism spread far and wide until it dominated the Prostestant thinking of Europe.

As a system of theology it was the most logical, consistent, and thorough statement of Christian doctrine ever given to the world; as a way of Christian life, it had many serious shortcomings.

The main beliefs and practices of Calvinism were as follows:

> God as all powerful.
>
> Man as utterly helpless before God.
>
> Salvation by election.
>
> A democratic church government.
>
> A Christian life, which was stern and somber, ethical and practical, being enforced by strict discipline.
>
> Baptism, as a seal as well as a sign of grace. He retained infant baptism, but only for children of Christian parents.
>
> Lord's Supper, where Christians received the spiritual flesh and blood of Christ, not the physical, as Luther believed.
>
> Heaven and hell as future resting places.

PROTESTANT GROWTH

Calvinism made a deep impression in Holland, Scotland, and England. As the result of the victories of William of Orange over Philip II of Spain, Holland became a "reformed" people with an established Calvinistic church under whose régime the country has flourished. Scotland, under the leadership of

John Knox, became a Calvinistic country in 1560, when the Scottish Parliament formally adopted the reform. The national church was called "Presbyterian," which became legally established under James, the son of Mary Stuart. The Anabaptist influence was very strong in England and gave rise to the Puritan movement from which many of our modern denominations have arisen. For a while Calvinism developed in France, but the Catholic opposition was too great. Thousands of Protestants were "butchered" by the Catholics on St. Bartholomew's night, in 1572. For a while the Protestants enjoyed peace under the Edict of Nantes, granted by Henry IV in 1598. But in 1685 persecution again broke out, the Edict was revoked, and the Protestant cause in France suffered a blow from which it has never recovered.

The "Wars of Religion" increased as the Protestants grew in number. The first war has just been mentioned under Henry III, that of Switzerland (1529 to 1531). In 1547 the Schmalkald War broke out in Germany, followed in 1551 by another in which the Protestants completely defeated the Catholics. During 1562 to 1598 both France and the Netherlands were being torn to pieces by religious wars. The most terrible of all wars of religion was the Thirty Years' War (1618 to 1648) in Germany.

Not only was Germany devastated by it, but France, England, and Sweden also suffered. It was ended by the famous Treaty of Westphalia. This treaty marks the point where the Catholics were ready to admit that they could never suppress the Protestants by the use of force. Though the struggle between Protestants and Roman Catholics has continued ever since, in many different forms all over the world, it has taken place mainly in the arena of theology, and not upon the battlefield.

THE ROMAN CATHOLIC CHURCH REFORMS

To keep abreast of the times the Roman Catholic Church realized that it must reform and thus regain its former power. So Pope Paul III summoned a General Council to be held at Trent on December 15, 1545. Here doctrines of the Church were defined, justification by faith condemned, the Church made equal to the Bible as an authority, the sale of indulgences abolished, and education for the clergy stressed.

Ignatius Loyola, a Spanish nobleman, was injured in both legs at the siege of Pampeluna (1523). While he was recovering from the wounds he conceived the plan of forming a monastic order composed of military men who would be at the service of the Church. At the University of Paris he gathered

a group of men and set out for the Holy Land
to do missionary work. But the road was blocked
and, upon their return to Rome, the "Society of
Jesus" was organized. Members took the regular
monastic vows, and in addition they took the vow
to go wherever the Church willed on a moment's
notice. They were militant in spirit and action, having
a general at Rome and officers throughout the world.
The society soon became the controlling force of
the papacy.

THE RISE OF DENOMINATIONS

The strict laws and practices of the Puritans resulted in a great reaction under Charles II (1630 to
1685). In the first place the Act of Uniformity
(1662) compelled almost two thousand Puritan clergymen to withdraw from the Church of England.
Conventicle and Five-mile Acts were passed which
deprived the Nonconformists of their special forms
of worship. It was not until 1689 that they were
granted their freedom by the passage of the Toleration Act, in the reign of William and Mary. Mean-
while many different sects had grown up.

The Conventicle Act of 1592 had driven the Separatists out of England and threatened them with
death if they returned. Most of these refugees made
their new homes in Amsterdam, Holland, where they
were welcomed and allowed to worship as they saw

fit. During the period of 1595 to 1620 many of these companies went to Holland, including such men as Henry Ainsworth, Francis Johnson, and John Robinson. The next chapter will deal with the Pilgrims, who left Holland to settle in the land of freedom.

3. VIRGIN TERRITORY
FOR THE CHURCH

MISSIONS

Columbus' discovery of America (1492) gave the Church a new hope—that of Christian missions. As Daniel Webster said: "It cannot be denied that with America and in America a new era commences in human affairs." All Europe wanted a share in this new and rich land. Spain sent out expeditions under such men as Ponce de Leon, Balboa, Cortez, DeSoto, and Coronado; English expeditions were led by Frobisher, Davis, Gilbert, and Raleigh; and the French made explorations along the St. Lawrence River, led by Jacques Cartier. In all these discoveries the Church had a large part. This was the period when England and Spain were bitter rivals. England, during Elizabeth's reign, was making a brave fight for the Protestant cause, while Spain under Philip II was still loyal to the pope. With every expedition from Spain, therefore, and also from Portugal and from France, a priest went in the name of the Church; in every English expedition a representative of the Church of England was included. As Henry

Rowe writes, in his *History of Religion in the United States:*

Spanish noblemen took with them their Catholic priests to plant the banner of the Cross alongside the banner of Spain, for their religion was a part of the equipment of their Latin civilization. . . . A century later French voyageurs into Canada took with them their confessors, and the devoted Jesuit missionaries pushed into the interior to propagate their faith among the natives of the North.

TRANSPLANTING DENOMINATIONS

As a result of the Reformation there sprang up, all through Europe, many sects or denominations. When immigrants came to America from different parts of Europe they brought with them their own particular belief. When the Dutch emigrated to New Netherlands, they took their Reformed Church with them; when Sweden sent her emigrants to Delaware, she also sent the Lutheran Church with them; when England established a permanent settlement in Virginia, she established the Church of England along with it. A little later English Puritanism found a place in New England, and the Presbyterians and Baptists established themselves in Maryland, Virginia, and the Carolinas. The English Quakers bought New Jersey, and the Methodists were found in America before they separated from the Church of

England. And in America these denominations found rich soil in which to grow.

VIRGINIA, THE NEW HOME OF THE CHURCH OF ENGLAND

It was in 1607 that English immigrants settled in Jamestown, Virginia. At first these colonists met with defeat on every hand, but with the help of their dauntless leader, John Smith, they finally won a measure of success.

This colony was governed by a body which was subject to a council in England under the control of the king. This council saw to it that the colonists did not forget their Mother Church. One article in the charter read "that the colonists should establish the Church of England as the only form of worship," and the governors saw that this was carried out. It is said that if a man refused to go to church he was put on a short allowance of victuals, and then whipped every day until he begged to hear the preaching once more. It must have been wonderful to be a preacher in those days!

This system, however, did not prove satisfactory. It was too far removed from the Mother Church to work effectively. Also, it lacked a bishop to confirm the young people and to ordain a native clergy. As the colonists were democratic in spirit this control

was a great hindrance to their growth. As Henry
Rowe says:

Far better it would have been to throw the colonial
churches on their own responsibility, permitting them to
grow vigorous through self-reliance.

NEW ENGLAND CONGREGATIONALISM

The Separatists, having withdrawn from the
Church of England because of its form of worship,
had formed independent congregations. Since they
were not able to obtain freedom in England, they
went to Holland (1607). Here they found a welcome, but realizing that they would soon lose their
very language and customs if they remained, they
decided to emigrate to America. On December 21,
1620, the good ship *Mayflower* sailed into Plymouth,
Massachusetts, harbor with one hundred and two
Pilgrims. It was not long before they had built log
huts for general use, had their own government, had
laws and were enforcing them, made treaties with
the Indians, bought out the English company,
farmed, fished, and traded. And so the colony grew.
"Sunday after Sunday they climbed the hill to the
log church, which was at once meetinghouse, fort,
lookout; lived as good neighbors during the week;
and acknowledged no ecclesiastical authority but
their own suffrages."

In this manner Congregationalism was planted in America—being the first denomination to break away from the old ecclesiastical order in the new land of freedom. Their courage and foresight paved the way for Puritan New England which gave to America its first lessons in stern justice, moral living, and aggressive business methods.

PURITANISM IN AMERICA

In 1630, a great emigration of Puritans to New England began under the direction of the Massachusetts Bay Company. John Winthrop, a wealthy Puritan, was made governor, and he with seven hundred of his kinsmen settled in and around Boston. During the next ten years 20,000 others followed and were "the very flower of the English Puritans." This colony had its own town meetings which Thomas Jefferson said were the "wisest invention ever devised by the wit of man for the perfect exercise of self-government." (Only members of the Puritan Church could vote.) Soon these people became engaged in fishing and shipbuilding, and thriving commerce with the West Indies resulted.

These people believed in education and said that "learning should not be buried in the graves of their fathers." In 1635 the Boston Free Latin School was built, the oldest English school in America. By 1647 the foundation of the common-school system in the

United States had been laid by the Puritans. It was in 1639 that the first English college was founded: Harvard College, at Cambridge, Mass. This began the line of Puritan institutions which was to extend across America.

RELIGIOUS EMANCIPATION

The Puritans had demonstrated the value of religious freedom, even if they had not always practiced it. After all, they had gone only halfway. It was left to Roger Williams to emancipate religion in America. He was the first person to put into practice the American principle, "that government has nothing whatever to do with maintaining any particular form of religious worship."

Having been driven from Massachusetts because of his religious views Roger Williams fled to the south with a few of his friends and settled in a land he called "Providence." Here he formed a colony which granted liberty to all, whether they were Protestants, Catholics, or Jews. It even protected unbelievers just as long as they behaved themselves. This idea of freedom grew gradually, although it was at first feared by the other colonies, until it became written into the Constitution of the United States in these words:

Congress shall make no law respecting an establishment of religion, or prohibiting the free exercise thereof.

No religious test shall ever be required as a qualification to any office or public trust under the United States.

History has honored Roger Williams by placing him in the ranks with Newton, Kepler, and Copernicus, as a modern benefactor to mankind. This is only a fair estimate of his worth when his contribution to America is considered.

4. THE ROMAN CATHOLIC CHURCH—
the church of authority*[1]

* Notes by chapters are found at the end of the book, beginning on page 124.

WHEN?

The history of the Roman Catholic Church may be traced through the successive bishoprics of Rome, alleged to start with St. Peter. This is the Church which recognizes the pope as the vicar of Christ on earth and the visible head of the Church.

WHERE?

The Roman Catholic Church was founded at Rome, which seemed to be the natural location for such an organization, both geographically and politically. It then extended its power westward, until it had a mighty following throughout all Europe.

Roman Catholic history in North America begins about A.D. 1125, when the first diocese was established in Greenland; and there were resident bishops until 1377. It was considered too cold in Greenland for any permanent settlement. A bishop-elect came along with Columbus to the New World. Sees were established in Haiti and Puerto Rico. In 1565 the first parish in the United States proper was founded, that of St. Augustine. Roman Catholic work was also developed about this time in Mexico. Seventy-five years after Columbus, the Roman Catholic Church was well established in America.

Most of the French explorers and colonizers of the sixteenth and seventeenth centuries were Roman Catholics. Missionary groups were also active. The vast province of France, which included the Mississippi valley along with Louisiana, came under the jurisdiction of the See of Quebec in 1674.

In 1634 Roman Catholics founded Maryland, which, according to Catholic historians, has the distinction of being the first English settlement where religious freedom was a part of the common law. Jesuits, from 1634 to 1773, worked in Maryland, Pennsylvania, and northern Virginia. In 1784, Father John Carroll was appointed Prefect-Apostolic of the Roman Catholic Church in the United States, and six years later became the first bishop of Baltimore, with jurisdiction over the entire country. From this time on, and particularly from 1828 to World War I, the growth of this Church was exceedingly rapid, owing largely to immigration.

WHY?

The Roman Catholic Church is the continuation in history of the Apostolic Church. It remained the principal Church of Christianity until the schism with the Eastern Orthodox Church in 1054. There has been no break in this organization from the very beginning to the present time, although during the Middle Ages it was shaken by corruption and moral decay. It has always renewed its spirit, however, and today is one of the most powerful and influential factors in the modern world.

WHAT—IN ORGANIZATION?

The Papacy. At the head of the Roman Catholic Church sits the bishop of Rome, who is Pope. His authority is supreme in all things concerning the Church. Next in order is the College of Cardinals, which acts as an adviser and head of commissions, called congregations. The cardinals elect the new pope in case of death, and many of them make their home at Rome.

A cardinal secretary at the Vatican serves as secretary of state. Permanent "congregations," each with a cardinal at its head, consist of The Holy Office, Consistorial, Sacramental Discipline, The Council, Affairs of Religion, de Propaganda Fide. Tribunals control the judicial functions of the

Vatican State. Besides the greater prelates there are bishops, priests, and deacons. The actual government of the Church here in the United States is represented by an apostolic delegate at Washington, D. C., cardinals, archbishops, bishops, diocesan clergymen, and members of various religious orders.

Appointments.   All appointees to bishoprics in this country are made by the Holy See at Rome, upon the recommendations of the hierarchy in the United States. No married person can hold an office in the hierarchy of the Roman Church.[2] Their two main reasons for this are that celibacy leaves them more free to perform their duties, and that continence is regarded as a more holy state than marriage.

Church Services.   The different services of the Roman Catholic Church are as follows:

> *High Mass,* where parts of the liturgy are sung by the officiating clergymen, and other parts by the choir.
>
> *Low Mass,* in which the priest reads all the parts.
>
> *Solemn Mass,* in which the priest is assisted by a deacon and subdeacon.
>
> *Pontifical Mass,* which is celebrated by a bishop and by certain other prelates.
>
> *Special services,* held on Fridays and on all holy days.

WHAT—IN BELIEF?

Since it is impossible to do justice to the history, practices, and doctrines of the Roman Catholic Church in such a limited amount of space as we have available here, we would strongly recommend that the reader secure such leaflets and booklets as the following, which give, in semipopular form, the position of this Church: *Introduction to Catholicism,* by Martin J. Scott; *Sixteen Steps to the Church; Five Great Encyclicals; The Faith of Our Fathers,* by James Cardinal Gibbons; and *The Faith of Millions,* by the Reverend Dr. John A. O'Brien. Also a reading of *My Sunday Missal* helps to give an understanding of the devotional side of Roman Catholicism.

These few quotations from the Catechism give a fairly good idea of what Roman Catholics are taught concerning:

The Virgin Mary. Original sin is not actual, but inherited. Our first parents, by their transgression of God's commandments, lost their high estate. . . . The Blessed Virgin Mary alone, of all human persons, was exempt from original sin, that is, from the first moment of conception, she possessed justice and holiness, namely, fulness of grace. That is the meaning of the Immaculate Conception.

Incarnation. The Incarnation means that the Son of God became man in the course of time. Christ was God from all eternity, and Man from the time of His human

birth. When it is said that God became man, it does
not mean that He was changed into man, but that as
God, He assumed human nature, so that in the one
person Christ, there are the two natures, the divine and
the human. This, like the Trinity, is a mystery of faith.

The Church. The Church is the congregation of all
those who profess the faith of Christ, partake of the
same sacraments, and are governed by their lawful
pastors under one visible Head.

The Pope. The Pope is the visible head of the Church
of which Christ is the invisible head. The Pope when
defining matters of faith and morals, has Christ's guaran-
tee that he will not err. This prerogative of the Pope is
called Papal Infallibility. It is divine assurance that when
the Pope in his official capacity, declares and defines
Christian dogma, he is immune from error.

The Sacraments. There are seven sacraments:
Baptism, Confirmation, Holy Eucharist, Penance, Extreme Unction, Holy Orders, and Matrimony. . . . A
sacrament is an outward sign instituted by Christ to
give grace. . . . The sacraments are not mere symbols,
but actually bestow grace, and hence were instituted by
Christ Himself, the possessor and origin of grace. No
human being has the power to institute a sacrament.

Baptism. Baptism is the first and the most necessary
of the sacraments. . . . Besides remitting sin, Baptism
confers sanctifying grace, making the baptized person a
child of God. By Baptism, all our sins, original and
actual, are forgiven; all punishment due to sin is remitted; our souls receive a mark or character which
will remain forever.

Forgiveness of Sins. By the sacrament of Penance,
Christ conferred on His Church the power to forgive
sins: "Whose sins you shall forgive, they are forgiven

them" (John XX, 23). By the absolution and penance given after confession, the guilt and eternal punishment of sin are remitted, and also part of the temporal punishment.

Transubstantiation. By the Consecration at Mass, the substance of bread and wine becomes the body and Blood of Christ. This change is termed Transubstantiation. . . . Ordinarily when the substance of a thing changes, there is a corresponding change of the accidents. But in the case of the Eucharist, the externals or accidents do not change with the change of substance. We have no perceptible evidence of the change. We believe it on the word of God. Hence the Eucharist is called a mystery of faith.

The Mass. The Mass is the renewal of the sacrifice of the Cross in an unbloody manner, the same as the first Mass, celebrated in anticipation, by Christ Himself at the Last Supper.

Extreme Unction. Extreme Unction is so called because it is administered as the last rite to the faithful. Like all the sacraments, it confers grace through the infinite merits of Jesus Christ. The dispositions of the recipient may affect more or less the spiritual benefits of Extreme Unction, but the grace of the sacrament is conferred even on those who are unconscious, provided they had the intention, at least implicitly, of receiving this sacrament with the proper dispositions when the necessity should arise.

Holy Orders. Holy Orders is the sacrament instituted by Christ in order to perpetuate the ministry of His Church. By this sacrament, bishops, priests and other clerics receive the power and grace to perform the sacred duties of their various ministries. The Catholic priesthood goes back in unbroken and valid ministries.

The Catholic priesthood goes back in unbroken and valid succession to Christ Himself. The Catholic priesthood, alone, recognizes the successor of Peter as the Vicar of Christ, the Chief Bishop of Christendom, the Rock on which the Church of Christ rests divinely secure.[3]

5. THE PROTESTANT EPISCOPAL CHURCH—
the church of beauty[1]

The Church of England was first planted in America by a chaplain of the exploring expeditions of Frobisher (1578) and Drake (1579). The charters, which Sir Humphrey Gilbert (1578) and Sir Walter Raleigh (1584 to 1587) had, provided for "public service according to the Church of England." Permanent worship was begun in 1607 by the Reverend Robert Hunt, at Jamestown, Virginia, when he celebrated the Eucharist beneath a large sail stretched between two trees. At first, toleration was shown to all, but as the Crown secured direct control over the colony harsh and rigid laws were prevalent in regard to Puritans and Quakers.

The first Episcopal Church in New England was King's Chapel in Boston, opened in 1689. During 1698 a church was established at Newport, Rhode Island, and also the Trinity Church in New York City was consecrated the same year.

There were two weaknesses in these first churches

in America: first, there were only a few established churches in the colonies and these aroused antagonism, for the colonists had no desire for a State-Church; and, in the second place, it was not possible to obtain competent ministers because they had to go to England to be ordained. Thus it was very difficult for the Mother Church to keep watchful care over the younger churches in America.

Samuel Seabury became the first bishop of the American Church in 1784. Elected to the office by the clergy of Connecticut, he was consecrated by the Scottish Episcopal Church. "Seabury House," headquarters of the present national organization, is named after him.

The first move toward independence was made in 1782, when the Reverend William White of Philadelphia published "The Case of the Episcopal Churches in the United States Considered," which urged the churches to form some kind of organization. The name "Protestant Episcopal" was first proposed by a committee at Annapolis in 1783 and adopted by the General Convention of 1789. The term "Protestant" was to distinguish it from the Church of Rome, and the word "Episcopal" was to distinguish it from the Presbyterian and the Congregational bodies. In the same year the *Book of Common Prayer*, the constitution, and canons were adopted.

The name of Dr. W. A. Muhlenberg should be mentioned in relation to this Church.

He founded the system of Church schools, organized the first free church of any importance in New York City, introduced the male choir, sisterhoods, and the fresh air movement; while his church infirmary suggested to his mind St. Luke's Hospital, the first church hospital of any Christian communion in the country.

The Protestant Episcopal Church has always been very active in the ecumenical movement and has contributed many outstanding public servants. Her missionary work has been a strong factor in the development of central administrative organizations. It also takes care of large areas of social service and community welfare work.

WHY?

The Protestant Episcopal Church is in the main the Church of England reborn in America. During the colonial period it was under the jurisdiction of the Bishop of London, but after the War of the Revolution it formed its own organization and became separate from the Mother Church. Yet, as the preface to the American *Prayer Book* states:

This Church is far from intending to depart from the Church of England in any essential point of doctrine, discipline, or worship.

WHAT—IN ORGANIZATION

System of Government.   This includes the parish, the diocese, the National Council, and the General Convention.

Officers of Parish.   The officers consist of a rector, who is also a priest; the wardens, who have charge of all records and the collection of alms; and vestrymen, who have charge of the church property.

The Diocese.   The government of the diocese rests upon the bishop and the diocesan convention, which meets annually. This convention is a self-governing body, but appoints a standing committee for all purposes declared by the General Convention. A bishop is elected by the diocese, but must be approved by a majority of the bishops and the standing committees of all the dioceses.

The General Convention.   This is the highest ecclesiastical authority in the Church. It consists of the House of Deputies, which is composed of delegates elected from the dioceses; and the House of Bishops, which includes:

. . . every bishop having jurisdiction, every bishop co-adjutor, and every bishop who by reason of advanced age or bodily infirmity has resigned his jurisdiction.

The two Houses vote and deliberate separately.

Every measure which becomes a law must be passed by both Houses.

A National Council was established in 1919, with a presiding bishop at its head. It acts as the executive body of the General Convention between sessions and has charge of general missionary, social, and educational work.

The Rector.   The rector is received according to diocesan law. His salary is cared for by the vestry of the local church. Some dioceses have endowment funds from which the salary of the rector is provided. The missionary bishops receive their salaries from the treasury of the Domestic and Foreign Missionary Society.

Lay Readers and Deaconesses.   These are appointed by the bishop of a diocese or missionary district, to assist in public services, to care for the poor and sick, and to instruct in religious education.

WHAT—IN BELIEF

Creeds.   The Protestant Episcopal Church adopts the Apostles' Creed and the Nicene Creed.

It expects of all its members loyalty to the doctrine, discipline, and worship of the one holy Catholic Apostolic Church, in all the essentials, but allows great liberty in non-essentials. There is no inclination to be rigid or to raise difficulties, but the fundamental principles of the church, based upon the Holy Scripture as the ultimate rule of faith, have been maintained whenever a question has arisen demanding decision.

Clergy.   The clergy make the following declaration:

I do believe the Holy Scripture of the Old and New Testaments to be the Word of God, and to contain all things necessary to salvation, and I do solemnly engage to conform to the doctrine, discipline, and worship of the Protestant Episcopal Church in the United States of America.

Baptism.   Baptism is by either immersion or pouring. Those who have been baptized as children are received into church membership through confirmation by the bishop, after having been instructed in the catechism of the Church. For those who were not baptized as children, admission is by baptism—either immersion, sprinkling, or pouring—and acceptance of the Apostles' Creed.

Communion.   This denomination places special emphasis upon the Lord's Supper, the "High Church" holding to a similar view as the Roman Catholics.

The Thirty-nine Articles.   The Thirty-nine Articles of the Church of England (with the exception of the twenty-first) were accepted in 1801 as a general statement of doctrine. They are added to the *Prayer Book,* but are not required as essential for either confirmation or ordination.[2]

6. THE UNITED PRESBYTERIAN CHURCH—
the church of duty[1]

WHEN AND WHERE?

The first Presbyterian churches in this country were established in Virginia, New England, Maryland, and Delaware. The first established was in Virginia. It resulted from the appointment of the Reverend Alexander Whitaker as pastor in 1611. There were also many Presbyterians among the first settlers of New England and in the church founded at Plymouth in 1620.

The first ecclesiastical gathering of an intercolonial and federal character was held by this denomination at Philadelphia in 1706. Here was formed a presbytery, but in 1716 the membership grew so greatly that a synod with four presbyteries was organized.

An "Adopting Act" was passed by the general synod, in 1729, by which it was agreed that all ministers of the synod should declare "their agreement in and approbation of the Confession of Faith with the Longer and Shorter Catechisms of the Assembly of Divines at Westminster." For a time

(1728 to 1758) there were two parties in the Presbyterian Church: the "Old Side" indorsing the intellectual attitude and the "New Side" indorsing the spiritual attitude. But in 1758 they agreed to adopt the Westminster Standards pure and simple, and were thus united.

During the years 1790 to 1837, the membership increased from 18,000 to 220,500. This was due chiefly to the religious revival which was sweeping the country at that time. Also the plan of co-operation with the Congregational Church, whereby ministers of one church were allowed to serve in the other, greatly added to the strength of this body.

Women have always had a voice in the government of this Church. They vote for pastor and other church officers, and also have their foreign missionary societies and educational work. Each church may also have deaconesses who are under the direction of the session.

Why?

The Presbyterian churches in America were mostly of English and Scottish origin, although they had no official connection with the churches of the mother country. Their pastors were mostly Church of England ministers holding the Presbyterian views which demanded a spiritually minded ministry and membership. This movement was the result of the influence of Calvin working in the Church of England.

WHAT—IN ORGANIZATION?

The Presbyterian Church has two basic factors: teaching elders or ministers as representatives of Christ, and the ruling elders as representatives of the people. The administrative system is made up of the *session*, which governs the congregation; the *presbytery*, which governs a number of congregations within a limited district; the *synod*, which governs the congregations of a larger district; and the *General Assembly*, which is the supreme judicatory.

The session has charge of the reception of members, discipline, and spiritual affairs of the church.

The presbytery has power "to receive, ordain, install, and judge ministers; to supervise the business which is common to all its congregations; to review session reports; to hear and dispose of cases coming before it on complaint or appeal; and to have oversight of general denominational matters."

The synod has the power "to review the record of its presbyteries, to hear and dispose of all complaints and appeals, to erect new presbyteries, to supervise within the administration of all denominational matters, and, in general, to care for its churches and ministers under the direction of the General Assembly."

The General Assembly. The General Assembly is the highest judiciary of the Church. It is composed of ministers and ruling elders from each presbytery, chosen in the following manner: "Each presbytery consisting of not more than twenty-four ministers shall send one minister and one elder, and each presbytery consisting of more than twenty-four ministers shall send one minister and one elder for each additional twenty-four ministers or for each additional twenty-four ministers or for each additional fractional number of ministers not less than twelve."

The duty of the General Assembly is to decide upon all controversies concerning doctrine and discipline; to erect new synods, to appoint boards and commissions; to receive and issue all appeals. Its decision is final, except in such cases as affect the constitution of the Church.

Church Membership. All candidates are examined by the session as to their Christian life and belief. An assent to the creed of the Church is not required. Both infants and adults are baptized by sprinkling, although in the latter case immersion may be substituted. The Church serves the Lord's Supper to all evangelical Christians. Those who worship regularly but are not members are called "adherents." Only communicants have the rights of full membership.

WHAT—IN BELIEF?

The Presbyterian's standards of belief are the Westminster Confession of Faith and the Larger and Shorter Catechisms. These were adopted in 1729. In 1886 a few alterations were made and a declaratory statement was adopted setting forth "the universality of the gospel offer of salvation, declaring that sinners are condemned only on the ground of their sin, and affirming that all persons dying in infancy are elect and therefore saved."

The fundamental beliefs[2] of the Presbyterian Church, based on Calvinism, are as follows:

> The sovereignty of God in Christ in the salvation of the individual.
> Each believer's salvation is a part of an eternal divine plan.
> Salvation is a spiritual gift from God and is not a reward for faith.
> Man is utterly unable to save himself.
> Regeneration is an act of God alone.
> Those who are once actually saved will always remained saved.

The Church insists upon the supreme importance of the spiritual life, but it gives both the minister and the laity full liberty to worship God as their consciences direct. The Presbyterians have stressed education and maintain a very high standard for the ordination to the Christian ministry. They also specialize in good preaching.[3]

UNION OF TWO BRANCHES

Two bodies of the Presbyterian faith, the Presbyterian Church in the U.S.A. and the United Presbyterian Church of North America, began in January, 1957, to vote on a possible merger. As a result of this, a uniting General Assembly was held in Pittsburgh from May 28 to June 3, 1958. A new denomination was created, to be known as the United Presbyterian Church in the U.S.A.

The Presbyterian Church in the U.S.A. dated from the first presbytery organized in Philadelphia in 1706. The first General Assembly was also held in Philadelphia (in 1789).

The other branch of the new merger, the United Presbyterian Church of N.A., was formed in 1858, when the Associate Reformed Presbyterian Church and the Associate Presbyterian Church united.

7. THE UNITED CHURCH OF CHRIST—
the church of vision[1]

(Congregational Christian Churches
Evangelical and Reformed Churches)

WHEN AND WHERE?

A new united Christian body was created June 25, 1957, in Cleveland, Ohio, when 700 delegates declared at a Uniting General Synod:

We do now, as the regularly constituted representatives of the Evangelical and Reformed Church and of the General Council of the Congregational Christian Churches, declare ourselves to be one body and our union consummated in this act, establishing the United Church of Christ in the name of the Father and of the Son and of the Holy Spirit. Amen.

WHY?

This merger marks the first time in American church history when two Protestant churches of different forms of government have united. The process of union was seventeen years in the making, and is not yet complete. Although both denominations were born during the Reformation, one has its roots in seventeenth century England while the other comes out of sixteenth century Germany.

As Puritans the Congregationalists sought the New World where they might enjoy freedom of conscience and worship as they pleased. All through the years since, Congregationalists have maintained and championed the independence and autonomy of the local church. This was continued in their union with the Christian Church in 1931.

The Evangelical and Reformed Church has been "presbyterian" in its polity ever since its earliest days in this country. At that time, in the early 1700's, groups of German farmers came here to settle rich farm land in eastern and southern Pennsylvania. This communion is also the result of a previous union, with the Reformed and Evangelical churches, which based its theological foundations on the Heidelberg Catechism and the Augsburg Confession.

WHAT—IN ORGANIZATION?

In outlining the chief points of the whole document the executive head of the Congregational Christian Churches, who is now co-president of the new body, explained that it provides that every Congregational church has a right to determine for itself whether it will become a part of the new body. In 1957 over 78 per cent of these churches had indicated their desire to join the United Church.

The document provides that not only will men

and women "enjoy the same rights and privileges" in the new church, but that "at least one-third of the members of national administrative bodies shall be women." This is thought to be the first time that any national church organization has gone on record with such a requirement.

The next step in the process of union will be the formation of a binding constitution. This is now in the hands of a commission of thirty persons and is expected to be completed by 1960. It must then be accepted by two-thirds of the member churches voting.

Speaking of the constitution the Evangelical and Reformed co-president said: "We must fashion a constitution which will be absolutely faithful to the principles of the *Basis of Union*. In doing so, we shall demonstrate that freedom is never jeopardized when order and community are agreed upon in love."

At the beginning few changes will be noted, at least during the two-year period, on the local level. Mergers, however, of national denominational boards will proceed, with both bodies pooling their resources and personnel. Even after the constitution is adopted, each church will remain free to own and manage its own property, call and dismiss its ministers, and carry on its own affairs as before.

The United Church of Christ brings together 1,400,000 Congregationalists with 5,600 churches, and 800,000 members of 2,730 Evangelical and Reformed churches. With a total membership of 2,200,000 it is the ninth largest denomination in the United States.

WHAT—IN BELIEF?

The foundation of the new union is a document entitled *The Basis of Union and the Interpretations*. The confession of faith of this union reads as follows:

In token of the faith which unites us, we unite in the following confession, as embodying these things most surely believed and taught among us:

We believe in God the Father Almighty, Creator and Sustainer of heaven and earth, and in Jesus Christ, his Son our Lord and Savior, who for us and our salvation lived and died and rose again and lives forevermore, and in the Holy Spirit, who takes of the things of Christ and shows them to us, renewing, comforting and inspiring the souls of men.

We acknowledge one holy catholic church, the innumerable company of those who, in every age and nation, are united by the Holy Spirit to God in Christ, are one body in Christ, and have communion with him and one another.

We acknowledge as part of this universal fellowship all throughout the world who profess this faith in Jesus Christ and follow him as Lord and Savior.

We hold the church to be established for calling men to repentance and faith, for the public worship of God, for the confession of his name by word and deed, for the administration of the sacraments, for witnessing to the saving grace of God in Christ, for the upbuilding of the saints, and for the universal propagation of the gospel; and in the power of the love of God in Christ we labor for the progress of knowledge, the promotion of justice, the reign of peace, and the realization of human brotherhood.

Depending, as did our fathers, upon the continued guidance of the Holy Spirit to lead us into all truth, we work and pray for the consummation of the kingdom of God; and we look with faith for the triumph of righteousness and for the life everlasting.

WHAT—IN PRACTICE?

The basic unit of the United Church of Christ is the congregation, or the local church. The congregations may, in turn, through their ministers and delegates elected from their membership, form themselves into Associations and Conferences. The Conferences constitute the General Synod.

The government of the United Church of Christ is exercised through these Congregations, Associations, Conferences, and the General Synod in such a way that the autonomy of each one is respected in its own sphere—each having its own rights and responsibilities. While the rights and responsibilities of these bodies will be further defined, the Basis of Union states that the rights formerly enjoyed by the local congregations shall in no wise be abridged. (See page 5 of the official document.) [2]

8. THE LUTHERAN CHURCH—
the church of faith[1]

WHEN AND WHERE?

The first Lutherans to settle in North America came from Holland to Manhattan Island in 1623. For many years they were not allowed to establish their own form of worship, for the authorities had received instructions "to encourage no other doctrine in the New Netherland than the true Reformed." But in 1674 the English took possession of New York and the Lutherans were granted full liberty.

The first independent colony of Lutherans was established in 1638 on the Delaware River by some Swedes sent over by the prime minister of King Adolphus. Reorus Torkillus was the first Lutheran minister to settle in the United States. This was in 1639. Soon afterward a church was built at Fort Christina, where he held services.

Other churches were established by Swedish and German immigrants in Pennsylvania, Delaware, Virginia, the Carolinas, and Georgia. By the middle of the eighteenth century Pennsylvania alone contained about thirty thousand Lutherans. The first synod, that of Pennsylvania, was organized by Muhlenberg (a man who took for his motto, "Ecclesia Plantand"), patriarch of the Lutheran Church in America, in 1748. The second synod, that of New York, was formed in 1786. By 1818, the growth of the denomination had become very rapid. In 1820, the General Synod was formed, mostly through the work of Schmucker, founder of the Gettysburg Theological Seminary.

This growth was due mostly to immigration from such Lutheran countries as Sweden, Norway, Denmark, Finland, and Germany. The larger proportion was composed of Germans. In 1918 different factors united to form the United Lutheran Church in America, the most notable exceptions being the Augustana Synod and the Missouri Synod.

Today the communicants of the Lutheran bodies in the United States number about seven million members. Throughout the world "Lutheranism represents about 47 per cent of Protestantism, and 5 per cent of the world population."

Why?

The Lutheran Church dates from the time of the Reformation. It can be said without causing too much opposition that Martin Luther was responsible for its origin. Although he had no intention of forming a denomination, the faith which bears his name has spread to the uttermost bounds of the earth in the form of the Lutheran churches. Therefore the spirit of the Protestant Reformation—that of dissatisfaction with the Roman Catholic Church and a strong belief in salvation by faith in Christ— still lives in the world in the form of the largest Protestant denomination in the world, with some 70 million members.

WHAT—IN ORGANIZATION?

For the most part the Lutheran Church is congregational in policy, especially when the authority of ecclesiastical bodies over the local churches is concerned. But for general administrative and consultative purposes it is representative.

The organization of the local church is composed of the congregation and a church council made up of the pastor and the church officers. The church officers are composed of elders and deacons, and sometimes trustees. When there are no trustees, the deacons take care of the temporal affairs of the church. Each church governs its own affairs according to its constitution.

Besides the local churches, there are conferences and synods. These vary in constitution and in form. Some have no ecclesiastical authority, but others have committed to them legislative authority and their action is recognized by the churches. For the

most part, the local church has the right to voice
its approval or disapproval in these matters. The
Lutheran Church has a liturgical form of worship
and observes the various general festivals of the
Christian church.

WHAT—IN BELIEF?

As it has already been said: know Martin Luther's
beliefs, and you will know the doctrines of the
Lutheran Church. In brief, these are the main con-
victions held by the Lutheran Church:

Justification is by faith alone.

The word of God is the only rule of faith.

The Lord's Supper is more than a memorial;
it is a channel of God's grace.

Baptism affords the potential gift of regeneration
from the Holy Spirit.

Infant baptism is regarded as proper and fitting.

The whole doctrine of this Church centers in the
gospel of Christ for the fallen man. This is summed
up in the Augsburg Confession. Dean Brown says
in regard to this Church:

The Lutheran Church is a liturgical church and it
exalts the value of the sacraments. But it does not allow
"the outward and visible sign of an inward and spiritual
grace" to interpose itself in any mechanical way between
the heart of the communicant and the Real Presence of
the Spirit abiding within the soul of the believer. "The

sole value of the sacrament," Luther taught, "is its witness to the divine promise. It strengthens faith. It seals or attests the God-given pledge of union with Christ and the forgiveness of sins."[2]

NATIONAL LUTHERAN COUNCIL

The National Lutheran Council, with headquarters at 50 Madison Avenue, New York City, is the service agency of the following Lutheran bodies: The United Lutheran Church, the American Lutheran Church, the Augustana Lutheran Church, the Evangelical Lutheran Church, the Lutheran Free Church, the United Evangelical Lutheran Church, the American Evangelical Lutheran Church, and the Finnish Evangelical Church.

It has departments covering the areas of American missions, the Lutheran World Federation, public relations, student service, welfare, military service, relief and refugee work.

9. THE REFORMED CHURCH
the church of concern[1]

WHEN AND WHERE?

Many were the denominations which sprang up as a result of the Protestant Reformation. Those which cannot trace their origin back to Luther can usually trace it back to Zwingli, Calvin, and Melanchthon. Of those which fall in the latter class there are the Reformed Church of Switzerland, Holland, and Germany; the Presbyterian Church of Scotland and England; the Huguenot Church of France; and the national churches of Bohemia and Hungary. All these represent nearly the same general movement.

When the Dutch and the Germans emigrated to America they brought the Reformed Church along with them. The first Reformed Church in America was that on Manhattan Island, which was organized by the Dutch, in 1628. Later some Germans, being driven from the Palatinate by the severe persecutions of Louis XIV, settled in upper New York and Pennsylvania. As immigration increased the Dutch made their headquarters in Michigan, where they could co-operate with the New York branch, which came to be known as "The Reformed Church in America." The German Reformed Church became "The Reformed Church in the United States."

At first these bodies held to their own language and customs. This, of course, checked the natural growth, and the practice was abandoned. Now the use of English has been accepted and this Church has become, to a great extent, Americanized. This body remains conservative, however. Yet it is a friendly Church and enters gladly into interdenominational relations. It has always had a missionary outlook and stands for the best in education and scholarship.

WHY?

What Martin Luther is to the Lutheran Church, so Zwingli and Calvin are to the Reformed Church. It had its beginning in Switzerland in 1516. Although it is contemporary with the Lutheran Church, it has no official connection with it. After the early death of Zwingli, John Calvin became the leader of this body. Because of Calvin's influence, it holds a very distinct type of Calvinistic doctrine and a presbyterian polity.

WHAT—IN ORGANIZATION?

The Reformed Church has a presbyterian type of organization. That is, the local church is controlled by a consistory which is composed of ministers, elders, and deacons who are elected by the members of the church. The ministers and elders attend to the spiritual affairs while the deacons care for the secular matters.

The local church organization differs from the presbyterian system in that the elders and deacons, the consistory, are the trustees.

The Reformed Church in America is governed by a General Synod which meets annually and has the following organizations: Board of Directors, Board of Domestic Missions (Church Building Fund), Women's Board of Domestic Missions, Board of Foreign Mission, Board of Education, Young People's Work, The Minister's Fund, and the United Advance Fund. It has many of the most historic colonial churches of New York and New Jersey.

WHAT—IN BELIEF?

The doctrine of the Reformed Church is represented in the Apostles', the Nicene, and the Athanasian creeds. Also the Canons of the Synod of Dort, the Belgic Confession, and the Heidelberg Catechism all contain statements of their belief. It is distinctly a Calvinistic body. Stress is placed upon liturgy.

Children are baptized "as heirs of the kingdom of God and of his covenant"; adults are baptized on profession of faith in Christ unto the remission of sins.

The church membership consists of all baptized persons. These are under the care of the Church, and are subject to its government and discipline. The prospective members do not sign any specific creed, but they are required to make a confession of faith before the minister and elders.

The Lord's Supper is practiced, with emphasis placed upon the spiritual presence of Christ at the Supper. Here is one of the chief differences between the Lutheran and the Reformed churches.

10. THE BAPTIST CHURCHES—
the churches of freedom[1]

WHEN AND WHERE?

There are some who say that the Baptist churches had their origin in the Apostolic Age. It has been said:

> Baptists began with the churches of the New Testament. They are not Protestants. They flourished down to the uniting of the Church and the State by the Emperor Constantine and continued through the Middle Ages in the secluded parts of Europe. They existed under various names, always, however, maintaining certain Baptist characteristics.

This statement may be true of the Baptists in a vague sense, but it is true of many other denominations as well. It is certain that a line of Baptist churches cannot be traced back to the Apostolic Church. The Baptist churches and Baptist principles are two different things.

The Baptist churches, as we know them today, are purely an English product. The first church of this denomination was established by a body of English refugees who settled in Amsterdam, Holland, in 1608. They were closely connected with the Congregationalists, led by Robinson and Smyth, in Holland. It was this John Smyth who established the church in Amsterdam. In 1611, Thomas Helwys returned to England with part of Smyth's congregation because they were unwilling to be united with the Mennonite Church as Smyth desired. They established the first Baptist church in England at London during the same year (1611).

There is a question in regard to the establishment of the first Baptist church in America. The honor very probably falls upon the church at Providence, Rhode Island, established by Roger Williams, in 1639, although the First Baptist Church of Newport, Rhode Island, claims this title, being founded in the same year by John Clarke. (We had better let the two churches settle this point for themselves.) But we may say that it was Roger Williams, the "Apostle of Religious Liberty," who was the founder and, for a while, leader of the Baptist movement in America.

There have been divisions in this denomination, such as the Primitive, United, General, Free. The largest body is now known simply as the "Baptists." This body includes the American (northern), Southern, and National (colored) Conventions. The divisions are largely for administrative purposes and imply no marked divergence either in doctrine or ecclesiastical order. When the strength of the Baptists is to be considered, all these bodies should be included. The Baptists of the whole world, numbering some twenty million, are united in the Baptist World Alliance.

There has been a very marked advance in the missionary activities, both home and foreign, during recent years.

WHY?

The Baptist churches are founded upon two great principles: personal liberty and freedom of belief. Smyth refused to accept infant baptism for the simple reason that it was in direct opposition to these beliefs. In the same way, Roger Williams refused to bow either before State or Church, and in so doing established a body of followers who recognized the Scriptures as their only rule of faith and discipline.

WHAT—IN ORGANIZATION?

The Baptist churches have an independent and congregational form of organization. Each church is a separate unit, having control over its own worship and discipline, the calling and dismissal of the pastor, the election of all church officers, deacons, and trustees.

A candidate for church membership is usually examined by a body of deacons in regard to his Christian experience and then voted upon by the members of the church. Admission to membership is preceded by baptism by immersion, although in some Baptist churches members from other churches are received who have not been immersed. The new member is required to sign no creed, but only to accept the New Testament as the sole guide in the religious life.

The officers of the church consist of the pastor, deacons, trustees, treasurer, and clerk, and sometimes a standing (or advisory) committee which is composed of the pastor and officials with several other members elected by the church. This committee has no authority except that granted by the members. The church property is generally held by a board of trustees, or it may be held either under the control of the entire society or of a special committee.

Ministers are licensed to preach by the church where they hold their membership. When ordination is desired, the candidate is brought before a council, called by the candidate's church, which is composed of selected members of sister churches. Here the candidate is questioned in regard to his religious experience, his call to the ministry, and his views on certain doctrines. When the candidate becomes a pastor he becomes a member of the church which he serves. He has no special authority and is under the discipline of the church which he is serving.

The churches unite in associations where reports

from the various churches are read and recommendations are made. These associations have no authority over the local churches and meet merely for mutual help. Besides these area associations there are state conventions, City Mission Societies, and various national missionary, educational, and pension boards. A national convention, which meets annually, is the top organization. These conventions of American (northern), Southern, and National (colored) Baptists have no authority over the individual churches.

WHAT—IN BELIEF?

Baptists have no creed; neither do they have any imposed statements of faith. As Dr. E. Y. Mullins has said:

No central authority speaks for Baptists. Their church and district associations usually announce certain cardinal truths of Christianity in order to define themselves. But these are never imposed upon others. They are merely testimonies to the way in which the Bible is understood and interpreted. They are not identical in meaning, although there has been remarkable unity among Baptists.

The two principal confessions are the Philadelphia Confession (1689) and the New Hampshire Confession (1832). Neither of these is a true statement of Baptist beliefs, nor in any way binding. All the Baptists are free to interpret the Scriptures as conscience directs, and a wide margin is set in which beliefs may be modified as new light comes through science and education. It is impossible, therefore, to define Baptist churches in so many words, because each church and each member is given the privilege to worship God through Jesus Christ with an open mind and a creative spiritual outlook.[2]

BAPTIST WORLD ALLIANCE

The Baptist World Alliance, with offices at 1628 16th St., N.W., Washington, D.C., is the fellowship and co-ordinating agency of 23 million Baptists around the world. It meets every five years. While it has no authority over other Baptist bodies, it does have such mutual service agencies as a world relief and refugee committee, co-ordinated youth and women's work, and has had a marked influence in the area of religious liberty.

Congresses have been held in London (1905), Philadelphia (1911), Stockholm (1923), Toronto, Canada (1928), Berlin (1934), Atlanta, Ga. (1939), Copenhagen (1947), Cleveland (1950), and in London for the second time (1955). The tenth Baptist World Congress will be held in Rio de Janeiro, Brazil.

11. THE QUAKERS—
the church of light[1]

WHEN AND WHERE?

George Fox, the founder of this "denomination," was born in 1624, at Leicestershire, England. The teaching which he emphasized—that of direct communication with God and the abolishment of all forms and creeds—was something new for his day. But soon he gathered a band of laymen who went all through England and Ireland teaching about the "inner light." They had no intention of establishing a new sect, but merely to win people to a more spiritual life. However, as their number increased a loose organization was formed called "The Children of Light." Later they called themselves the "Religious Society of Friends," and were commonly called "Quakers."

These Friends were severely persecuted in England, chiefly because they refused to attend the services of the Established Church, to pay tithes, to take oaths, or to fight in war. Many of these were fined, and not a few were cast into jails; yet persecution did not put out the "inner light" of these friendly people. On the contrary, Rountree reports:

During the Commonwealth, and throughout the reign of Charles II, the Friends were constantly growing in number in England and in other countries, and by 1690 were a numerous as well as a well-organized people.

The first Friends, or Quakers, to arrive in this country (Massachusetts) were Ann Austin and Mary Fisher (1656), but they were taken for witches and sent back to Barbados whence they came. For many years severe laws were put upon the Quakers and they were treated without mercy. However, they began to increase in America, and at last found a welcome in Rhode Island. They were also to be found in New York, New Jersey, and Maryland; but the far greater number settled in Pennsylvania under William Penn.

WHY?

The Society of Friends is the result of a yearning in the hearts of many English people for a more spiritual type of Christianity. These people protested against all ecclesiasticism, sacramentarianism, and traditionalism, and demanded a more ethical and practical religion. As Rountree states, it was their hope that:

. . . all Christian people might come to obey the light of Christ in their own hearts, and that so great a reformation, social as well as religious, might be wrought through Christendom.

These Seekers found in George Fox a trusty leader, and under his guidance have given the modern world a demonstration of true religion.

WHAT—IN ORGANIZATION?

The worship of the Friends is based upon three verses of Scripture: first, "God is a Spirit, and they that worship him must worship in spirit and in truth" (John 4:24); second, "Where the Spirit of the Lord is, there is liberty" (2 Corinthians 3:17); and third, "Let all things be done decently and in order" (1 Corinthians 14:40). Therefore, they meet in silence at a stated hour, they have no sacred building, and all are free to take part in the meeting if they are so led by the "inner light."

They do have "church" officers—elders and ministers—who are selected by the members because of their special calling. It is the duty of the elders to have charge of the conduct of the public worship, while the minister cares for the spiritual matters. There is, however, no line of distinction drawn between the laity and the clergy, for they hold that all Christians are ministers or priests. When a member has especial ability to speak and to give spiritual help he is usually recommended for the ministry (women may become ministers as well as men). They usually receive no salary and continue to work at the ordinary tasks at which they were formerly engaged. There are a few who form a separate class, however, such as those occupied with full-time religious service at home and abroad. These have their living expenses paid by the Society.

The Society is governed by a series of meetings: preparative (congregational), monthly, quarterly, and yearly. In these meetings any member of the Society is free to take part. There is no voting, but decisions are arrived at through the "sense of the meeting." When a diversity of opinion is felt by the clerk of the meeting, the assembly is adjourned until some later date.

The business of the monthly meeting is to receive and exclude members, to care for the poor and the education of children, to appoint church officers, to liberate ministers for religious service, to appoint registering officers, overseers, and elders.

The quarterly meeting is composed of all the monthly meetings within a certain district and its business is partly devotional and partly executive. The yearly meeting is the unit of authority, and every member of the Society belongs to this body and all are equally free to speak.

Marriage, to the Friends, is a religious ordinance as well as a civil contract. Therefore, when a couple desire to get married, they go before a meeting and

mutually promise to be faithful to each other as
husband and wife. Thus they are wed.

WHAT—IN BELIEF?

The Friends have no creeds nor sacraments. They
will not take oaths; neither will they fight. They
dress simply and talk plainly. It is their purpose to
cultivate the "inner light" and to make God a vital
experience.

They believe supremely in the nearness of God to the
human soul, in direct intercourse and immediate communion, in mystical experience in a firsthand discovery
of God. . . . It means and involves a sensitiveness to
the wider spiritual Life above us, around us, and within
us, a dedication to duty, a passion for truth, and an
appreciation for goodness, an eagerness to let love and
the grace of God come freely through one's own life, a
reverence for the will of God wherever it is revealed in
past or present, and a high faith that Christ is a living
presence and a life-giving energy always within reach of
the receptive soul.—RUFUS JONES.

12. THE METHODIST CHURCH—
the church of action[1]

The great religious movement today known as
Methodism developed out of the uncertainty and desire for change in eighteenth century England plus
the personal spiritual experience of John Wesley.

John Wesley (born in 1703) the son of a rector in
the Established Church, trained at Oxford, early in
life sought Christian perfection. He became the leader
at Oxford of the Holy Club, comprised of his brother
Charles, George Whitefield, and other serious-minded
students. The purpose of the club was to study the
classics and devotional works, to help the poor, and
to minister to those in jail.

Seeking perfection through Christian service, John
Wesley spent two years (1735–37) in the new American colony of Georgia, along with his brother
Charles. His intention was to be a missionary to the
Indians. This mission, however, was not too success-
ful. But he did come in personal contact with a group
of Moravians, who were German refugees, and from
them he learned many lessons in faith and dedicated
Christian living.

BEGINNING OF A NEW LIFE

When Wesley returned to England in the spring of 1738 he was a troubled man. He was not satisfied with his own life. He felt that the Established Church was not meeting the social, moral, and religious needs of his own day.

On May 24, 1738, after attending a service in St. Paul's Cathedral, Wesley joined a few of his friends at a meeting house in London on Aldersgate Street. Here his heart was "strangely warmed." He says, in speaking of this great spiritual experience, "I felt I did trust in Christ, Christ alone for salvation; and an assurance was given me that he had taken away my sins, even mine, and saved me from the law of sin and death."

This deep religious experience marked the beginning of not only a new man but also of a new kind of religious movement. With a newly gained power John Wesley became the leader of a vast revival. He organized a corps of lay preachers, and he adopted on a large scale the practice of outdoor preaching to the masses. His brother Charles wrote beautiful hymns, and great choirs sang their way all over England, Wales, Scotland, and North Ireland.

In spite of the fact that religion was becoming alive again, the Church of England did not look with favor upon the enthusiastic movement. The Bishop of Bristol informed Wesley that he was not commissioned to preach in the area of his diocese. Wesley replied, "Woe is me if I preach not the gospel wherever I am in the habitable world." To another clergyman he said, "I look upon all the world as my parish."

METHODISM COMES TO AMERICA

A local preacher, Philip Embury, organized the first American group of Methodists. This was done in New York in 1766, in response to the urging of his cousin Barbara Heck. From a little group meeting in Embury's house the congregation grew until it was able to establish a church on John Street. This group soon thereafter sent an appeal back to England for help. In 1769 assistance was sent to the new world when the conference in England sent Richard Boardman and Joseph Pilmoor to New York as missionaries. They also sent along a contribution of fifty pounds to the new chapel. From 1769 to 1774 Wesley sent eight missionaries to America. In addition to Boardman and Pilmoor there were Francis Asbury and Richard Wright (1771), Thomas Rankin and George Shadford (1773), James Dempster and Martin Rodda in 1774. There were also several volunteers.

Another chapel was built by Robert Strawbridge at Sam's Creek in Maryland.

Asbury soon became the acknowledged leader of

the Methodists in America and "was destined under God to influence and shape the growing Methodist connection in America more than any other man."

The Methodist Episcopal Church was formerly organized in Baltimore during the last week of December, 1784. This famous "Christmas Conference" placed its stamp upon the entire development of Methodism in America. The name it adopted indicated that the church should be Methodist in doctrine and discipline, but Episcopal in its form of church government. It adopted a ritual for its various services which Wesley had sent over, and also a series of Articles of Religion which the present church still holds. This book was an abridgment of the *Book of Common Prayer* of the Church of England; and although free of the Established Church, its worship and ritual had its continuing influence. This conference also elected two men as bishops—Francis Asbury and Thomas Coke. They were first called superintendents, but within a few years the title of Bishop was adopted. Along with them twelve other men were ordained ministers and empowered to administer the Communion.

During its years of growth The Methodist Church has had to pass through several periods of division. But in 1939, in Kansas City, Missouri, the divisions of Methodism—the Methodist Episcopal Church, the Methodist Episcopal Church, South, and the Method-

ist Protestant Church—united to form The Methodist Church. This was the most significant act of
church union ever achieved in the United States.

WHAT—IN BELIEF?

Basic to Methodist belief is the document known
as the Articles of Religion. They were selected by
John Wesley from the Thirty-nine Articles of Religion of the Church of England. From the beginning,
and even to the present day, these Articles of Religion set forth in a formal way the Methodist faith.
They are a part of the Constitution of the Church,
and are published in its *Discipline*. Not even the
General Conference is allowed to change them. They
can be altered only by a long and drawn-out process
of amending the constitution. Methodists interpret
the Articles freely; nevertheless they serve as the
fountain of truth for each new generation.

Discipline is an important word in the Methodist
cause. It concerns what a Methodist is supposed to
do, and not do. The General Rules, published in the
book of *Discipline* and originally drawn up by John
Wesley, provide a systematic guide for Christian conduct. The negative rules include against the taking of
the name of God in vain, against profaning the Lord's
day, against drunkenness, against slaveholding, against
"the buying or selling goods that have not paid the
duty," against usury, against uncharitable conversa-

tion, against extravagance in dress, against diversions "as cannot be used in the name of the Lord Jesus," against harmful reading, against self-indulgence, against "laying up treasure upon earth," and against taking chances in financial matters.

Positive rules are: the practice of kindliness and Christian charity; helping those in need; to do good to the bodies and souls of men; mutual Christian helpfulness; diligence and frugality; patience.

Religious duties are: attendance at public worship; reading the Word; partaking of the Lord's Supper; family and private prayer; searching the Scriptures; fasting or abstinence.

What—in Organization?

Although the largest denomination, The Methodist Church is a rather closely knit organization. The basic unit is the local church or "charge." A charge consists of one or more local churches. If it is only one church, it is a "station"; if two or more, it is a "circuit."

Charges are grouped geographically first into districts supervised by a minister known as a district superintendent; secondly, districts compose the Annual Conference presided over by a bishop; thirdly, the Annual Conferences are grouped into six Jurisdictions.

The General Conference. The supreme governing

and lawmaking body. It meets every four years. It is composed of ministers and laymen in equal numbers, all elected as delegates by the Annual Conference.

Jurisdictional Conference. This is a new feature in Methodism. In 1939 five regional jurisdictions were created on a geographical basis, and one other on a racial (Negro) basis known as the Central Jurisdiction. The main duty of each Jurisdictional Conference is to elect the bishops and jurisdictional representatives on the general boards and agencies, and to plan and promote the general work of the Church for the next four years in its territory.

Central Conferences. These are in effect Jurisdictional Conferences outside the United States and its territories.

Annual Conference. This is the basic body of Methodism. It is composed of all ministers (called traveling preachers) who live within a certain territory, and of lay members—one of whom is elected from every charge in the conference area. Ministers when once admitted to an Annual Conference become members of it for life. They are known as "traveling preachers" and must be appointed to some charge or agency by the bishop. They may be transferred from one Annual Conference to another, with their consent, but no minister can be refused an appointment as long as he is a member of an Annual Conference. The Annual Conference is responsible for the good character and work of its ministers, and for the work of its various churches and institutions—colleges, hospitals, homes.

District Conference. It is held at least once a year in every district superintendent's area if the Annual Conference containing that district so orders. It is presided over by the district superintendent and gives him the opportunity to check up on the progress of the work of his district; it also takes final action on the licensing of properly qualified persons to preach.

Quarterly Conference. This is the governing body of the local church or charge, meeting quarterly and presided over by the district superintendent, who is the connectional link with the church at large. It is composed of the officials of the local church—pastor, assistant pastors (if any), stewards, trustees, local preachers (if any), superintendent of church school, president of the Woman's Society of Christian Service, and other specified officers.

Official Board. This is the real administrative body of the local church. It is a "must" in every church and meets monthly. Composed of the pastor, trustees, stewards, and certain other officials, it serves as the pastor's cabinet and supervises the total church program, carried out through commissions on missions, education, membership and evangelism, stewardship, social concerns, and sometimes others.

Judicial System. This is a unique feature of The

Methodist Church. The *Discipline* has a complete judicial system of law. Proper trial of church members and ministers is provided for when charges affecting their character or official actions are brought before the pastor, district superintendent, or bishop in a formal manner. A Committee of Appeals is created in each jurisdiction to pass upon cases referred to it. The supreme court of Methodism is the Judicial Council. It has the power to rule on the constitutionality of any act of the General Conference or of any Methodist agency. It also hears appeals from a bishop's decision and deals with questions of Methodist law. There is no appeal from the Judicial Council's decision. It sits during sessions of the General Conference, as well as at other stated times.[2]

13. THE UNIVERSALIST CHURCH—
the church of harmony[1]

WHEN AND WHERE?

The Universalist denomination is of modern origin. It is confined mostly to America and embraces only a portion of those who hold Universalist views.

This denomination began with the arrival of John Murray, of London, in Good Luck, New Jersey, in September, 1770. He preached in New York, Pennsylvania, and Massachusetts and as a result societies sprang up in these states which held to the Universalist view. A church was built by Murray at Gloucester, Massachusetts, in 1780. The name selected for this church was "the Independent Christian Society, commonly called 'Universalists.'"

The first convention of this body was held at Oxford, Massachusetts, in 1785; at this time little was accomplished outside of making a move toward a definite organization. The second convention was held in Philadelphia, in 1790. Here was drawn up and published the first Universalist profession of faith, an outline plan of church organization was made, and the convention approved the congregational form of polity. The third convention was held at Oxford, in 1793, and this developed, as years passed, into the Convention of the New England States and finally into the present organization, the general convention. In 1870 a plan of organization and a manual of administration were adopted which the denomination still uses.

WHY?

All true Christians believe that "God is love." The Universalists, however, could not make this belief coincide with the Calvinistic God and so they rejected the latter emphasis altogether. They preach a message of forgiving love as the central quality of divinity. And as Henry Kalloch Rowe says:

Enough of them had thus reacted against the hopeless doctrines of predestination and future punishment to organize Universalist churches.

WHAT—IN ORGANIZATION?

The Universalist Church has adopted the congregational form of organization. Each local parish or society is free in the management of its own temporal affairs, in conducting its worship, and in the choice of officers, including the pastor. The different parishes are organized into state conventions and

delegates from the state convention compose the
general convention.

In the *Organization and Administration Manual
for Universalist Churches* the following statement is
made regarding the general organization:

Historically, our church is a pure democracy; but its
polity is congregational. First come the parishes or
churches which voluntarily unite in state or national
conventions and delegate to these whatever powers they
possess.

By such process our church organization has come to
be constituted, on the same plan as the United States of
America, as follows:

The general convention, having jurisdiction over all
Universalist clergymen and denominational organization.

State conventions, exercising within state or provincial
limits a similar jurisdiction, subject to the general
convention.

Individual churches, composed of persons organized
for religious improvement and the support of public
worship.

Church Membership.   The admission to membership is not the same in all churches. But, on the
whole, the uniform custom is to require the Winchester Profession or the Statement of Essential
Principles as basic historic symbols. Most of the
churches have a covenant, but much freedom is given
the individual as to his interpretation of it.

Sacraments.   This   denomination   observes   the

Lord's Supper four times a year. Baptism is either by immersion or sprinkling, and is administered both to infants and adults. Both of these sacraments are used only as symbols. Only ordained ministers are permitted to administer these sacraments.[2]

WHAT—IN BELIEF?

The Universalist Church has no creed, but at the general convention held at Winchester, New Hampshire, in September, 1803, a profession of faith was formulated. This was accepted by the convention, but without ecclesiastical authority. However, today it is acknowledged by the denomination at large as an expression of its faith. It is as follows:

We believe that the Holy Scriptures of the Old and New Testaments contain a revelation of the character of God and of duty, interest, and final destination of mankind.

We believe that there is one God, whose nature is Love, revealed in one Lord Jesus Christ, by one Holy Spirit of Grace, who will finally restore the whole family of mankind to holiness and happiness.

We believe that holiness and true happiness are inseparably connected, and that believers ought to be careful to maintain order and practise good works; for these things are good and profitable unto men.

14. THE UNITARIAN CHURCH—
the church of reason[1]

WHEN AND WHERE?

Unitarianism of today originated in the first half century of the Protestant Reformation. During the sixteenth century many independent thinkers of Italy and Switzerland, along with a few Anabaptist leaders, held to the Unitarian belief.

In England there were such men as Newton, Locke, and Milton who held Unitarian views, but no move toward forming a distinct denomination was made until late in the eighteenth century.

In America, Unitarianism resulted from a division in the Congregational Church. This Church had left its members free to believe as they pleased; requiring no set doctrine, but only a short and simple covenant. As doctrinal changes arose, many of the churches in eastern Massachusetts slowly moved toward the Unitarian beliefs. In the second half of the eighteenth century, many of the most important and oldest churches accepted these beliefs. However, the first church completely to accept the new doctrines was King's Chapel at Boston, in 1785. At first these churches were called "Liberal Christians," but later (1815) the name "Unitarian" became attached to them.

The real cleavage between the Congregational and the Unitarian bodies took place when Henry Ware was elected professor of theology at Harvard University, in 1805. More and more the "liberals" were refused fellowship in the Congregational churches. When William Ellery Channing of Boston preached a sermon at Baltimore, in 1819, which defended and defined the Unitarian point of view, it was accepted as their platform.

On May 25, 1825, a missionary and promotion organization was formed which was called the American Unitarian Association. This made the Unitarians a separate denomination. In 1865, a national conference was organized and the period of aggressive denominational life was begun.

WHY?

To answer this question it will be very fitting to give Channing's definition of the true Church. He says:

By his Church our Saviour does not mean a party bearing the name of a human leader, distinguished by a form or an opinion, and on the ground of this distinction, denying the name and character of Christians to all but themselves. . . . These are the true church—men made better, made holy, virtuous by his religion—men who, hoping in his promises, keep his commands.

WHAT—IN ORGANIZATION?

The Unitarians have a congregational form of organization. Each church is separate and independent. For the purpose of fellowship and mutual counsel they meet in local, state, and general conferences. The International Congress attempts

. . . to open communication with those in all lands who are striving to unite pure religion and perfect liberty, and to increase fellowship and co-operation among them.

The minister is elected by the congregation. There are denominational officers, but no hierarchy. Each local church sends delegates to the American Unitarian Association and is thereby controlled by the churches.

Unitarians have no foreign missions as such, but they do have world-wide service projects. The Unitarian Service Committee, for example, serves all races, colors, and classes, giving medical aid, educational services, social welfare and direct relief.[2]

WHAT—IN BELIEF?

Unitarians have no creed. The constitution of the general conference states:

These churches accept the religion of Jesus, holding in accordance with his teaching that practical religion is summed up in the love to God and love to man.

The general consensus of their belief can be put in the following points:

The unipersonality of God.

The strict humanity of Jesus.

The perfectability of human character.

The natural character of the Bible.

The ultimate salvation of all souls.

Nothing is better, in order to understand the beliefs of this denomination, than *Leaflet 15,* published by the British and Foreign Unitarian Association.

Clayton R. Bowen, in *Why Are Unitarians Disciples of Christ?* makes Christ seem real when he says,

Jesus is our Leader, because he walked in the same path we must tread; our Master, because we cannot choose but to follow him; our Example, because we have similar divine possibilities; our Brother, because we have the same Father. . . . We take his hand because he is one of us.

Call him not heretic whose works attest
His faith in goodness, by no creed confessed.
JOHN GREENLEAF WHITTIER

15. THE CHRISTIAN CHURCH—
the church of unity[1]
(Also known as Disciples of Christ)

WHEN AND WHERE?

During the revival movements in the early part of the nineteenth century there arose people who stood for the Bible alone, without the aid of creeds or formulas. Thomas Campbell, a member of the Secession branch of the Presbyterian Church in Ireland, was one of the leaders of this group. He came to the United States in 1807 and settled in western Pennsylvania. Finding many people in this section without any direct church affiliations he invited them to join in his services. As a result, he and his son, Alexander Campbell, formed an organization called the "Christian Association of Washington, Pennsylvania." However, it was not the wish of these leaders that this association might become a distinct denomination, for denominations to them were "a horrid evil, fraught with many evils."

Because of their disbelief in infant baptism the Baptists had a great liking for this Christian fellowship. Upon the invitation of the Redstone Baptist Association, Alexander Campbell and his followers entered this organization in 1813, thus becoming a part of the Baptist denomination. But Mr. Campbell did not get along very well with his Baptist friends. His paper, the *Christian Baptist* (1823), caused widespread opposition against him, and henceforth Baptist churches began to disaffiliate his followers. Mr. Davis, the historian for the Disciples, says:

No exact day can be named as the time of this sad occurrence [the separation], for it came about gradually and consumed several years in its consummation; but we may date it 1830. After this the followers of Mr. Campbell were called Christians, or Disciples of Christ, or the Christian Church, the legal title being the Church of Christ at such and such a place.

The growth of this body has been very rapid especially in Ohio, Tennessee, and Missouri. The period directly after the Civil War was one of great expansion. It now ranks high in the list of Protestant denominations.

Why?

This denomination believes in restoration rather than reformation. It was the desire of this body, in the first place, to restore primitive Christianity, with all its beliefs and practices. It maintained that:

. . . nothing ought to be received into the faith or worship of the Church nor be made a test of communion among Christians that is not as old as the New Testament.

Therefore, since the Disciples could not agree with the sectarian spirit of the Church or with the creeds and beliefs it had made, they purposed to return to the pattern of the first church, as found in the New Testament.

WHAT—IN ORGANIZATION?

The Disciples' churches are congregational in organization. Each church elects its own officers and has entire control over its own organization. There is no outside ecclesiastical authority.

Candidates for membership are received upon profession of faith in Christ, before the pastor and congregation. Baptism by immersion follows.

The church officers are pastor, elders, and deacons. The duty of the elders is to care for the spiritual interests, while the deacons care for the financial affairs and the benevolences of the church.

Ministers are ordained by the local church.[2] The service is conducted either by the pastor or the elders, and sometimes by a committee from neighboring churches. The minister is a member of the church in which he is pastor or evangelist. Ministerial associations are formed for mutual help and general supervision, but they have no authority.

WHAT—IN BELIEF?

In general, the beliefs of the Disciples can be summed up in the following points:

Feeling that "to believe and to do none other things than those enjoined by our Lord and His Apostles must be infallibly safe," they aim, "to restore faith and spirit and practice the Christianity of Christ and His Apostles as found on the pages of the New Testament."

Affirming that "the sacred Scriptures as given by God answer all purposes of a rule of faith and practice, and a law for the government of the church, and that human creeds and confessions of faith spring out of controversy and, instead of being bonds of unity, tend to division and strife," they reject all such creeds and confessions.

They place especial emphasis upon "the Divine Sonship of Jesus, as the fundamental fact of Holy Scripture, the essential creed of Christianity, and the one article of faith in order to receive baptism and church membership."

Believing that in the Scriptures "a clear distinction is made between the law and the gospel," they "do not regard the Old and New Testaments as of equally binding authority upon Christians," but that "the New Testament is as perfect a constitution for the worship, government, and discipline of the New Testament Church as the Old was for the Old Testament Church."

While claiming for themselves the New Testament names of "Christians," or "Disciples," "they do not deny that others are Christians or that other churches are Churches of Christ."

Accepting the divine personality of the Holy Spirit through whose agency regeneration is begun, they hold that men "must hear, believe, repent, and obey the gospel to be saved."

Repudiating any doctrine of "baptismal regeneration" and insisting that there is no other prerequisite to regeneration than confession of faith with the whole heart in the personal living Christ, they regard baptism by immersion "as one of the items of the original systems," and as "commanded in order to the remission of sins."

Following this apostolic model, the Disciples celebrate the Lord's Supper on each Lord's Day, "Not as a sacrament, but as a memorial feast," from which no sincere follower of Christ of whatever creed or church connection is excluded.

The Lord's day with the Disciples is not the Sabbath, but a New Testament institution, consecrated by Apostolic example.

The Church of Christ is a divine institution; sects are unscriptural and unapostolic, and the sect name, spirit, and life should give place to the union and co-operation that distinguished the church of the New Testament.[3]

A "PECULIAR PEOPLE"

The Disciples call themselves a "peculiar people." This does not mean that they consider themselves odd or as standing off from others, but because they yearn for unity and for full Christian fellowship. They not only believe in Christian unity; they claim to have found the path to unity—in the restoration of simple New Testament Christianity. Says Dr. A. T. De Groot, "What was distinctive was our grand principle in restoration which gives us our validity in the Christian world today. Obscured from time to time by the fire and cloud of local battles, it commanded the minds of our greatest (Disciple) leaders."

16. OTHER IMPORTANT RELIGIOUS BODIES

THE EASTERN ORTHODOX CHURCH[1]

Just as it is impossible to do justice to any of the religious bodies noted in this chapter because of the limitation of space, so it is impossible to tell in any detail here the history and beliefs of the great Eastern Orthodox Church. Although it is in no sense connected with the Protestant Reformation, having separated from the Roman Catholic Church in A.D. 1054, it has played an important part in recent ecumenical conferences and has a close fellowship with Protestant churches.

It claims to be the one true church, founded by Christ and having its physical beginning in the first century with the Apostles themselves. It is now composed of national bodies, such as the Church of Russia, the Church of Greece. These Churches are independent of each other in their administration but at the same time are in full communion with one another. They all have the same faith, doctrine, Apostolic tradition, sacraments (seven), liturgies, and holy services.

The Orthodox Churches derive their teaching from two sources: the Bible and the sacred Tradition (both of equal value). Their creed is the Nicene Creed chiefly; their highest ranking clergymen, the Bishops, have no authority over each other. Archbishops, Metropolitans, Patriarchs are honorary titles, indicating spheres of jurisdiction. Orthodox Churches do not accept the doctrine of Papal Infallibility nor that of Papal Supremacy. It is therefore not in communion with the Roman Catholic Church.

The Adventists

The Adventists are a body of people who believe in the personal return of Christ to this earth some time in the near future. William Miller, at one time a Baptist, founded the movement in Massachusetts, in 1831. As the result of Miller's unfulfilled prophecies, concerning the second coming of Christ, the body became divided into six divisions, each holding the same views as formerly but setting no exact date for the return of Christ.[2]

The most important division of this body is the Seventh-day Adventists. This branch was organized in New Hampshire, in 1844, by some of Miller's followers. It is now organized into conferences with annual meetings. Stressing diet and health, it has built a number of sanitariums, one of the most outstanding being at Battle Creek. Membership is drawn from most of the states, and missionary work is conducted in Europe, Asia, Africa, and Australia.

Church of the Brethren

The Church of the Brethren grew out of the Pietistic Movement, being founded in Schwarzenau, Germany, in 1708. As a result of persecution, because of its opposition to the formal religion of the state churches, a congregation came to Germantown, Pennsylvania, in 1719 and established a church. From there the movement spread to the west and the south.

It is an extremely democratic church, with all members having an equal vote. Delegates are sent to annual district conferences and the General Conference. The church has no creed, but accepts the New Testament as its rule of faith and practice. It holds that only willing believers are to be baptized by immersion, that no member should take part in war, that all should live a simple life and be temperate, that class distinctions are wrong, and that right living is superior to creeds. It has distinguished itself by its extensive world relief program, particularly in its origin of the Heifers for Relief project.[3]

The Christian Scientists

This denomination was founded in 1876 by Mary Baker Eddy. Its first church—the First Church of

Christ, Scientist, in Boston—was organized in 1879. This became the "Mother Church" of many branch churches which were founded, both in America and Europe, especially in the large cities.

The services of this church consist of readings from the *Bible* and from Mrs. Eddy's *Science and Health*, hymns, prayers, and the benediction. At the midweek service testimonies and experiences are given. There are no pastors, but instead two Readers, namely: the First Reader (of *Science and Health*) and the Second Reader (of the *Bible*). The "Galilean Breakfast" takes the place of the Lord's Supper.

Mrs. Eddy's book, *Science and Health*, is the basis for the belief of this body. It is the "key" to the Scriptures. It reveals unto man the science of God, the only Reality.

One of the most remarkable achievements of this body is the publication of *The Christian Science Monitor*, recognized as one of the best daily newspapers of the nation.

EVANGELICAL UNITED BRETHREN CHURCH

This denomination had its birth at Johnstown, Pennsylvania, on November 16, 1946, when the consummation of organic union between the Evangelical Church and the Church of the United Brethren in Christ took place. Jacob Albright was the founder of the former, and Philip William Otter-

bein of the latter. Both churches had their beginnings
in Pennsylvania, in the evangelistic movement of the
early nineteenth century. The government of this
denomination is Methodistic and its doctrine
Arminian.

The Evangelical United Brethren Church has a
constituent membership in the United States and
Canada of approximately 743,200, with an additional
125,000 in the mission field abroad. There are some
4,370 churches and 2,574 ministers. Under the basis
of union no changes have been made in doctrine.

PENTECOSTAL BODIES

Many relatively small organizations hold Pentecostal views, particularly those of sanctification and
holiness. Among the most important of these are
the Pentecostal Fire-baptized Holiness Church, the
United Pentecostal Church, Incorporated, the International Pentecostal Assemblies, the Pentecostal Assemblies of the World, the Pentecostal Church of
God in America, the United Pentecostal Church,
Incorporated, the Calvary Pentecostal Church, Incorporated, the Pentecostal Holiness Church, and the
Pilgrim Holiness Church.[4]

JEHOVAH'S WITNESSES

Though not organized into a formal denomination,
Jehovah's Witnesses are well known throughout the

world for their refusal to salute the flag, to partici-
pate in war, and their insistence that all their members have the official standing of ministers. In all
these matters they have taken their case to the Supreme Court of the United States.

Although not a sect or denomination, Jehovah's
Witnesses are associated with the Watch Tower Bible
and Tract Society, and with the International Bible
Students Association. Pastor Charles T. Russell was
their first leader. Upon his death, in 1916, Judge
Joseph F. Rutherford became president of the organization. After Judge Rutherford's death, in 1942, he
was succeeded in office by Nathan H. Knorr.[5]

The Mormons, or the Latter-day Saints

Joseph Smith founded this body April 6, 1830, at
Fayette, Seneca County, New York. His reason for
doing it was that the Lord had told him that all the
churches were wrong and that the true gospel would
soon be revealed unto men. Three years after this
experience an "angel" had come to him, while he
was in prayer in his room, and revealed to him
(September 22, 1827) the hiding place of some gold
plates on which was written the true word of God.
With the aid of certain supernatural "stones in silver
bows" his vision was clear to translate what was
written on the plates. When the work was finished
the plates were returned to the angel and the *Book*

of Mormon was published. It has fifteen divisions, each claimed to have been written by a different hand, which gives the history of certain imaginary races which once lived in prehistoric America.

After Smith's death the organization divided, but the largest part followed the leadership of Brigham Young. Under his guidance the organization was transferred to Great Salt Lake, Utah, where it has since remained.

REORGANIZED LATTER DAY SAINTS

The Reorganized Church of Jesus Christ of Latter Day Saints, with international headquarters in Independence, Missouri, claims to be the true successor of the church founded by Joseph Smith. It rejected the leadership of Brigham Young and formed its own organization at Beloit, Wisconsin, in 1852, with Joseph Smith, son of the founder of Mormonism, as the president. From the beginning it repudiated polygamy, and lays stress upon the continuity of divine revelation, the open canon of the Bible, the restoration of Christ's true church on the basis of the New Testament, the principle of Christian stewardship, and the practical application of Christianity to all phases of life.

THE MENNONITES

This body is the successor of the Anabaptist movement. Menno Simons, a converted Roman Catholic

priest, was their leader; and he successfully organized
the scattered congregations of the Anabaptists in the
Netherlands and Germany. In America the Men-
nonites first settled in Pennsylvania (1683), and
ever since this state has been their greatest strong-
hold.

The Mennonite Confession of Faith contains such
doctrines as the Trinity, the fall of man, the atone-
ment, nonresistance, the forbidding of the use of
oaths, baptism to believers by pouring, the Lord's
Supper observed twice a year, foot washing, and the
"kiss of peace." Holding office and the bearing of
arms for the State is also discouraged.

Bishops or elders exercise administrative oversight in districts and the pastors are chosen from the
congregation which they are to serve, sometimes
by lot. Deacons are chosen in the same manner.

The *Yearbook of American Churches* lists the fol-
lowing branches of the Mennonite faith: Beachy
Amish (26 churches); Church of God in Christ
(Mennonite) with 33 churches; Conference of the
Evangelical Mennonite Church (19 churches); Con-
servative Amish Mennonite Church (67 churches);
Evangelical Mennonite Brethren (20 churches); Gen-
eral Conference Mennonite Church (206 churches);
Hutterian Brethren (26 churches); Krimmer Mennon-
ite Brethren Conference (10 churches); Mennonite
Brethren Church of North America (71 churches);

Mennonite Church (840 churches); Old Order Amish Mennonite Church (240 churches).

THE MORAVIANS

This organization traces its history back to John Huss, the Moravian reformer, who was burned as a "heretic" at the Council of Constance, in 1415. Count Zinzendorf of Saxony became their protector and leader in 1722, and under his influence the "Brethren's Church" became reorganized, after the Thirty Years' War. Ten years later this Moravian Church launched a world-wide program of foreign missions.

The Moravian Church was first planted in America by immigrants in 1735, in Georgia. Later settlements were made in Pennsylvania, North Carolina, and Ohio. Here they did active missionary work among the Indians.

The Moravian Church subscribes to the Apostles' Creed and uses a variety of liturgies. It practices infant baptism. It has a membership of about 60,000 in America.

The organization is divided into two Provinces, each administered by a synod. In doctrine, Moravians emphasize the love of God, the second coming of Christ, his divinity, resurrection, prayer, and the inner testimony of the spirit. Moravians are noted for their beautiful outdoor Easter services.

The Nazarenes[6]

This body is the result of the fusion of several Holiness Associations in the eastern part of the country, the Church of the Nazarenes (in California), and the Holiness Church of Christ, which took place in 1907. This Church has been closely connected with the Methodist movement, both in type of organization and in belief. It has its general assembly, general superintendents, elders, and evangelists. In doctrine, it lays emphasis on the depravity of the human race, on entire sanctification, and on the second coming of Christ. It opposes the use of alcoholic drinks and tobacco, and membership in secret societies. It has its international headquarters in Kansas City, Missouri.

The Salvation Army[7]

The Salvation Army was founded in London in 1865, when William Booth began services for the unchurched masses in a "tent" erected in Whitechapel Road, East London.

The Army founder's first thought was to conduct a mission only, sending the converts to the churches. But to this there were three main obstacles: (1) They would not go where they were sent. (2) They were not wanted when they did go. (3) He soon found that he wanted them himself—to assist him in winning others of their class. He thus felt compelled to found a separate agency—the East London Christian Mission, later renamed The Christian Mission, ultimately to become The Salvation Army (1878).

In the early years General Booth realized the need for a much more precise form of adherence to the organization on the part of its members than he had at first anticipated. This need became evident in two particular directions: (1) doctrine, (2) individual effort. Every prospective member is thus required to sign "Articles of War," a declaration containing a profession of personal experience of salvation, a pledge of separation from the world and of loyalty to Jesus Christ, a pledge of allegiance to the Salvation Army, and a pledge of total abstinence from the use of all intoxicating liquors and baneful drugs.

In 1880 began the expansion of work in lands other than Great Britain; Salvation Army service in America was inaugurated in that year. At present it is at work in many countries and colonies, where its program of Christian evangelism and of Christian social aid to depressed peoples is universally accepted as a great social force.

JEWISH CONGREGATIONS[8]

Many hundreds of books have been written on the faith and practice of the Jewish religion. We include this brief section merely in terms of fraternal greetings and to indicate that the religion of the Old Testament is very much alive today in the various Hebrew congregations.

Jews arrived in the colonies some time before 1650. The first congregation is recorded in 1656, the Shearth Israel of New York City. The congregational and rabbinical organizations at the present time are the Union of American Hebrew Congregations, the Union of Orthodox Jewish Congregations, the United (Conservative) Synagogue of America, the (Reformed) Central Conference of American Rabbis, the Rabbinical Assembly of America, the Rabbinical Council of America, the Union of Orthodox Rabbis of the United States and Canada, and the Synagogue Council of America.

17. WORKING TOGETHER—
the denominations in co-operative action

The denominations are co-operating to a far greater extent than most people realize. In hundreds of communities throughout the nation they hold union services, have united relief appeals, and work through a council of churches. This is also true on area and state levels. Most of us are aware of the fact that young people, laymen and women, have many joint projects and programs which break over denominational lines. But the place where the largest amount of actual co-operation is being accomplished is on the national level, and it is here that it is the least understood.

HISTORICAL BACKGROUND

The movement of denominational co-operation in this country began in the area of Christian education. Sunday school workers held their first interdenominational convention, under the auspices of the American Sunday School Union, in 1824. The first national Sunday school convention was held in

Philadelphia in 1832. It was therefore the desire on the part of Christian laymen which brought the various denominations together into a working relationship.

In 1872, at the first international Sunday school convention which met in Indianapolis, plans and basic principles were adopted for a system of Sunday school lessons for the churches of America. In 1910 the Sunday School Council was organized, which paralleled the International Sunday School Association. At Kansas City, in 1922, these two bodies were united to form the International Council of Religious Education, which in 1950 became one of the divisions of the National Council of Churches. The World Council of Christian Education and Sunday School Association, although a separate body, works closely with these American agencies.

WORLD MISSIONS

Interdenominational co-operation also has been manifest in the field of world missions. After various expressions of united efforts, by 1910 the time was ripe for the great, historic conference held in Jerusalem in 1928. Then came the "Life and Work" conferences of Stockholm in 1925 and at Oxford in 1937. The other phase of this missionary co-operation had an expression in the term "Faith and Order," and this led to world conferences at

Lausanne in 1927 and Edinburgh in 1937, and at Oberlin, Ohio, in the fall of 1957.

At Jerusalem the term "younger churches," meaning the "new" churches largely of Asia and Africa came into use. By the time of the Madras Conference, in 1938, almost half of the delegates came from these so-called younger churches. The same emphasis was repeated at Willingen in 1952. These conferences were held under the auspices of the International Missionary Council, which is now being merged with the World Council of Churches.

Out of the "Life and Work" and the "Faith and Order" conferences came a desire for closer co-operation. In 1938, at Utrecht, Holland, a provisional constitution was adopted for a World Council of Churches. Because of World War II this remained "in process of formation," and it was not until 1948, in Amsterdam, that the World Council was fully organized. At the second assembly of the World Council, held at Evanston, Illinois, in 1954, the 163 member communions declared that they would not only "stay together" but also "grow together."

Missionary Co-operation

In this country, as a result of the will to co-operate, the Foreign Missions Conference was organized in 1893, and the Home Missions Council, the Missionary Education Movement, and the Federal Council of Churches came into being in 1908. In the meantime home mission bodies, state councils of churches, and local federations of churches began to spring up. The first of these was the International Commission of Maine, organized in 1891. The Federation of Churches and Christian Workers in New York City was created in 1895. It had for its purpose "to bring the intelligence and love of our churches to bear upon the material, social, economic, civic, and spiritual interests of the family life in our city, through interdenominational conference and co-operation to meet its every religious and moral need."

The student Christian movement has enlisted, trained, and sent out to the far places of the earth a host of young people who have been committed to the ecumenical principle. The YMCA and the YWCA have also trained many leaders and have brought Christian people together throughout the world in united programs.

Christian women have long thought in terms of Christian co-operation. Beginning with the Female Society for Missionary Purposes, at Boston in 1800, they have developed through hundreds of local organizations for worship, study, and action into the National Council of Federated Church Women (1929), the Council of Women for Home Missions and the Federation of Women's Boards of Foreign

Missions, and the United Council of Church Women which became a division of the National Council of Churches when it was organized in 1950 at Cleveland, Ohio.

Councils of Churches

The development of Christian co-operation is well illustrated in the growth of state, city, and county councils of churches. In 1912 a survey revealed a few such organizations and in 1915 there were only twelve salaried executives of such federations of churches and some of these were on a part-time basis. But by 1922 the real importance of such united bodies was realized. From that time on, paid executives began to head state, county, and local councils. The growth has been steady until now the term "tremendous expansion" has been applied to it. Today there are 40 state councils with paid secretaries, and only seven states lack some kind of an interdenominational organization of churches. Every state has a council of church women. There is a total of 318 state and local (city or county) organizations with paid staffs. In addition to this there are approximately 611 operating with voluntary leadership. Councils of church women now number over 2,000. And there are also over 2,000 ministerial associations. These, in turn, often become local councils of churches.

THE NATIONAL COUNCIL OF CHURCHES

The National Council of Churches is a voluntary fellowship of thirty-three major churches (denominations or communions), with a total of more than 38,000,000 members. It represents a practical expression of the unity of spirit and purpose which Christian people have because of their common loyalty to Christ, even though they belong to different denominations and creeds. Moreover, the Council is not a body apart from the churches, but is the churches themselves doing together what they believe can be done better unitedly than separately.

The various member denominations represent most of the major historic bodies of American Christianity. (The Eastern Orthodox Churches, but not the Roman Catholic, are included.)

Created in 1950 the National Council combines the work of the following former interdenominational agencies: Federal Council of the Churches of Christ in America, Foreign Missions Conference of North America, Home Missions Council of North America, International Council of Religious Education, Missionary Education Movement of the United States and Canada, National Protestant Council on Higher Education, United Council of Church Women, United Stewardship Council, Church World Service, Inc., Interseminary Committee, Protestant Film

Commission, Protestant Radio Commission, and the Student Volunteer Movement.

Offices of the National Council are located at 297 Fourth Avenue, New York 10, New York; 116 South Michigan Avenue, Chicago 3, Illinois; 122 Maryland Avenue, N.E., Washington, D.C.; and 63 Auburn Avenue, N.E., Atlanta, Georgia.

The greatest material symbol of Christian co-operation is found in the Interchurch Center on upper Riverside Drive, New York City. In this new building is to be housed not only all the departments of the National Council of Churches, but also many of the service agencies of several denominations. Interdenominational organizations like the Japan International Christian University Foundation will also be located here. As the Interchurch Center, with its many committee rooms, chapel and assembly halls, gets into full operation, the cause of Christian co-operation will be greatly advanced both in the ideal and in practice.

NOTES BY CHAPTERS

Chapter 4. *The Roman Catholic Church*
1. Approximately 35,846,500 members in the United States, according to the *Yearbook of American Churches.*
2. Marriage is permitted to certain Eastern Rite priests.
3. See *Primer on Roman Catholicism for Protestants* by Stanley I. Stuber (New York: Association Press).

Chapter 5. *The Protestant Episcopal Church*
1. Approximately 2,965,137 members in the United States.
2. Booklets entitled *The Episcopal Church* by Walter Herbert Stowe; *Tell Us About the National Council;* and *The Episcopal Church, Some Interesting Facts* may be secured from the National Council, Protestant Episcopal Church, 281 Fourth Avenue, New York 10, N.Y. Also *The Book of Common Prayer* is all-important in the understanding of the Protestant Episcopal Church.

Chapter 6. *The United Presbyterian Church*
1. Approximate membership in U.S.A.: Presbyterian U.S.A., 2,775,500; Presbyterian U.S., 848,750; United Presbyterian (now part of United Presbyterian U.S.A.), 257,520.
2. See *Calvin, A Life,* by Emmanuel Stickelberger, published by John Knox Press, Richmond, Va.
3. See also *A Brief History of the Presbyterians* by Lefferts A. Loetscher (Board of Christian Education,

United Presbyterian Church, U.S.A., Philadelphia, Pa.). This book contains a valuable bibliography.

Chapter 7. *The United Church of Christ*
1. Combined membership 2,192,674. (Congregational Christian Church, 1,392,632.)
2. See *Historical Sketches of The Congregational Christian Church and the Evangelical and Reformed Church; The United Church of Christ; The Basis of Union;* all may be secured at 257 Fourth Avenue, New York 10, N.Y.

Chapter 8. *The Lutheran Church*
1. Approximate membership in U.S.A.: United Lutheran Church of America, 2,235,500; Lutheran Church—Missouri Synod, 2,150,230; Evangelical Lutheran Church, 1,058,730; Augustana Synod, 576,190; American Lutheran Church, 910,011.
2. See leaflets "We Lutherans," "Lutherans Believe" by Walton H. Greever; "Like A Mighty Army" by Frank S. Mead; and the article "What Is a Lutheran?" by G. Elson Ruff, in the February 23, 1954, issue of *Look* magazine.

Chapter 9. *The Reformed Church*
1. Approximate membership in U.S.A.: Reformed Church in America, 213,550; Christian Reformed, 221,970. The Evangelical and Reformed Church is now part of the United Church of Christ, Chapter 7.

Chapter 10. *The Baptist Churches*
1. Approximate membership in U.S.A.: American Baptists, 1,536,280; Southern Baptists, 8,956,760; Negro Baptists, 7,226,215 in the two National Conventions.
2. See *The Baptist Story* by Robert G. Torbet; *Baptist*

Beliefs by E. Y. Mullins; *The Baptist Witness* by
Henry K. Rowe and Robert G. Torbet.

Chapter 11. *The Quakers*
1. Approximate membership of various bodies of Friends
   in the U.S.A., 120,000. See *Yearbook of American
   Churches* for brief history of these several divisions.

Chapter 12. *The Methodist Church*
1. Approximate membership of The Methodist Church
   in the U.S.A., 9,543,250; African M.E., 1,166,301;
   African M.E. Zion, 761,000.
2. See *The Discipline of The Methodist Church; Understanding The Methodist Church* by Nolan B. Harmon;
   A Short History of Methodism by Umphrey Lee and
   William Warren Sweet; *Inside Methodist Union* by
   James H. Straughn; and *The Methodist Way of Life*
   by Gerald Kennedy.

Chapter 13. *The Universalist Church*
1. Approximate membership in the U.S.A., 70,520.
2. See *The Beginnings of the Universalist Church* by A.
   Gertrude Earle; also *Charter and By-Laws* of the
   Universalist Church; *Religion Can Make Sense* by
   Clinton Lee Scott; *The Faith of a Universalist;* leaflets
   Four Year Advance, The Universalist Church (Uni-
   versalist Publishing House, 16 Beacon St., Boston 8,
   Mass.).

Chapter 14. *The Unitarian Church*
1. Approximate membership in U.S.A., 96,800.
2. See leaflet *Unitarianism: Some Questions Answered*
   by A. Powell Davies, and *Introducing Unitarianism*
   published by American Unitarian Association, 25
   Beacon St., Boston 8, Mass.

Chapter 15. *The Christian Church (Disciples)*
1. Approximate membership in U.S.A., 1,943,600.
2. Now "Christian Churches" officially as of 1956.
3. See article, "Who are the Disciples of Christ?" by James E. Craig, *Look* magazine, November 30, 1954; article, "Disciples of Christ" by Gaines M. Cook, *National Council Outlook,* June, 1953; special articles in January 4, 1959 issue of *The Christian Evangelist* and *Front Rank;* and Church Life series Pamphlet Library, published by the United Christian Missionary Society, 222 S. Downey Ave., Indianapolis, Ind.

Chapter 16. *Other Important Religious Bodies*
1. Eastern Orthodox membership in U.S.A., 2,540,450.
2. The Church of God is an important Adventist group. It represents churches holding premillennial views organized (1921) into a general conference with headquarters in Oregon, Illinois.
3. See *Minutes of the Annual Conference of the Church of the Brethren.*
4. See *General Constitution and By-Laws, The Pentecostal Church of God in America.*
5. See current *Yearbook of Jehovah's Witnesses* (Watch Tower Bible and Tract Society, Brooklyn, N.Y.) Also 1958 *Report of the Divine Will International Assembly of Jehovah's Witnesses.*
6. Approximately 282,000 members.
7. Approximately 250,000 members. See *The History of the Salvation Army* by Robert Sandall, 2 vols. (Nelson); *The Salvation Army Handbook of Doctrine; What Is the Salvation Army?,* published by the Salvation Army Printing Dept., New York, N.Y.
8. Jewish population in U.S.A., 5,500,000. See current *Yearbook of American Churches* for listing of various Jewish denominations, as well as social and educational agencies.